THE BADGER GAME

MICKEY McGUIRE TO AL TOON

TOM BUTLER

Design & Production
Dale J. Ver Voort

Cover Photos by L. Roger Turner

Published by William C. Robbins
at Straus Printing Company, Madison, Wisconsin

For book sales and other information, write the Promotions and Community Activities Department, Madison Newspapers Inc., P.O. Box 8056, Madison, Wisconsin 53708.

Personal notes may be mailed to Thomas J. Butler,
Madison Newspapers, P.O. Box 8056, Madison, Wisconsin 53708.

ISBN 1-878569-08-2

To Bonnie,
who kept home, hearth and five kids
(Terry, Kathy, Jeff, Jayme and Peggy)
going through all those crazy
newspaper hours.

ON THE COVER

1. *Alan Ameche's 1954 Heisman Trophy*
2. *Elroy Hirsch's 1946 College All-Star jersey*
3. *Vintage Football*
4. *Pat Richter's 1962 Knute Rockne Lineman of the Year Trophy*
5. *Action photo of Billy Marek*
6. *Hirsch's College All-Star helmet*
7. *1963 Rose Bowl program*
8. *Wisconsin Booster Button*
9. *Photo of Captain Robert "Red" Wilson and Coach Ivan Williamson in 1949*
10. *"Red" Wilson's 1949 Big Ten Most Valuable Player Trophy*
11. *Wisconsin's 1984 football brochure*
12. *Wisconsin leather helmet from the 1930s*
13. *Ameche on the cover of Parade magazine on September 5, 1954*
14. *Rose Bowl sideline pass*
15. *Modern Badger helmet*

TABLE OF CONTENTS

INTRODUCTION	1
MICKEY McGUIRE	5
THE FULLBACKS	9
PAT HARDER	15
ELROY HIRSCH	19
THE TOUCHDOWN TWINS	27
JUG GIRARD	31
ROBERT "Red" WILSON	37
THE HARD ROCKS	43
"THE HORSE"	51
HARLAND CARL	59
"HACK"	65
ALUMNI GAMES	73
PAT RICHTER	79
RON VANDERKELEN	89
THE ROSE BOWL	97
THE DROUGHT	103
RUFUS FERGUSON	109
BILL MAREK	117
THE ALL STARS	127
MIKE KALASMIKI	131
JESS COLE	137
THE WRIGHT STUFF	143
"STONY"	151
AL TOON	155
THE LINEMEN	161
ALL-TIME TEAM	167
THE LAST HURRAH	173
ONE MAN'S OPINION	179
INDEX	183

Introduction

"We didn't aspire to emulate Red Grange or Bronko Nagurski. We imitated Mickey McGuire. I became hooked on Wisconsin football..."

— *Tom Butler*
Author

The University of Wisconsin was one of seven charter members of the Intercollegiate Conference of Faculty Representatives, which subsequently has been called the Western Conference, the Big Ten, the Big Nine and eventually the Big Ten again.

James H. Smart, president of Purdue University, called a meeting of the presidents of seven universities at Chicago in 1895 to consider a blueprint for regulating and controlling intercollegiate athletics. Besides Wisconsin, the original seven included Chicago, Illinois, Michigan, Minnesota, Northwestern and Purdue.

A year later one faculty representative from each of the seven schools met at the Palmer House in Chicago and the conference was born Feb. 8, 1896. Indiana and Iowa were added in 1899.

The Western Conference operated with nine teams from 1900 until 1908 when Michigan withdrew in protest against "retroactive provisions of certain conference enactments."

Ohio State was admitted in 1912 and Michigan resumed its membership in 1917. Chicago discontinued its football program in 1940 and withdrew from the conference formally in 1946. Michigan State was admitted in 1949 and started basketball competition in 1950-51 and football in 1953. Usually everyone referred to the conference as the Big Ten, though, not the Big Nine.

Wisconsin has a rich football tradition. It's part of the campus fabric and indeed even that of Madison each autumn. When the air gets a little crisper and leaves turn to flame, excitement mounts around the old Civil War training ground called Camp Randall.

I first sensed this tradition while listening to my grandfather talk about Pat O'Dea and Eddie Cochems and when my dad recounted the exploits of Eddie Gillette, Keckie Moll, Cub Buck and Rollie Williams.

Born and reared in Madison, I first grasped the fun and fancy of this Wisconsin tradition as a youngster on the East Side when I noticed accounts in newspapers and on radio about a charismatic UW halfback from Hawaii named Walter "Mickey" McGuire.

As kids playing football on sandlots, we didn't aspire to emulate Red Grange or Bronko Nagurski. We imitated Mickey McGuire. I became hooked on Wisconsin football, even though the 1930s can hardly be considered a "golden era" for the Badgers.

The late 1930s and early '40s, though, were great years for UW athletics. John Walsh developed the country's premier college boxing teams, Chuck Fenske and Walter Mehl campaigned as world class middle distance runners, Bud Foster's 1941 basketball team won the school's only NCAA championship in that sport and in 1942 Harry Stuhldreher fielded his finest football team and arguably the school's best ever.

When I was in the Navy during World War II and some of my shipmates found out I came from Wisconsin, so many wanted to know about John Kotz, Pat Harder and especially "just how good is this guy 'Crazylegs' Hirsch?"

I have a special affinity for the 1942 football team because I was a freshman at the university that fall and the Badgers developed into the finest UW football team in 30 years. The electricity around Camp Randall on game days and the excitement throughout the city was greater than anything I'd seen in my life up to then and possibly never has been surpassed.

While I was overseas, my dad mailed me the Wisconsin State Journal sports page practically every day. That's how I learned about the heroics of a 17-year-old halfback named Jug Girard as well as the exploits of Jerry Thompson and Don Kindt. He also sent an overseas subscription to The Sporting News. I think all these newspapers piqued my interest in sports writing.

This book contains one man's reflections after observing approximately 60 years of Wisconsin football, including 37 as a sports reporter and columnist, 25 in close contact with UW football as my major "beat" for the Wisconsin State Journal.

The University of Wisconsin does have a rich football tradition, not a winning tradition to the extent of Michigan and Ohio State, but a longer association with the Intercollegiate Conference of Faculty Representatives than either of those schools.

Wisconsin has won only seven conference football championships, three since 1952. The Badgers probably could be considered perennial "bridesmaids" because they finished second 10 times and on 15 occasions they came within one victory of capturing a title. Badger fans always have exhibited exceptional loyalty through triumphs, near-misses and those periodic downturns that tested their resolve.

Although the Big Ten remains the Intercollegiate Conference of Faculty Representatives, certain UW faculty members through the years have not always shown strong support for its football program and occasionally actual disdain.

Through times of triumph and trial I always have been impressed by the dedication of a series of beleaguered coaching staffs as well as the resolve and commitment of hundreds of young men preparing for and playing the games.

Some critics question the worth of a university-sponsored intercollegiate athletic program and football in particular. But, I've concluded that, although a university can operate famously without football, the sport does enhance a school's image and college life. Football provides a valuable diversion and a rallying point for students, alumni and even ordinary fans with little or no association with the school. More importantly, the sport provides a healthy outlet for young men with a craving for competitive athletics.

I'm confident an overwhelming majority of those with whom I've had contact at Wisconsin consider their participation in Badger football a positive university experience.

Society likes to identify with something — a church affiliation, a lodge, a club, an athletic team. Badger football, which started more than a century ago, remains a favorite tradition to thousands in Wisconsin.

This book features many of the individuals I've known or covered through 60 years and recounts the exploits that made them Badger football favorites and in some cases Wisconsin legends.

Tom Butler

Mickey McGuire

"Mickey fought his way the remaining three yards for a touchdown with Gophers hanging onto his legs and riding his back."

— *1932 Newspaper Article*
Reporter Unknown

University of Wisconsin football "began" in 1932 with Mickey McGuire because that's when the author first discovered the school on the shores of Lake Mendota does enjoy a gridiron tradition and many athletes who played the game on the fields of Camp Randall did become legendary.

Pat O'Dea, who became immortal because of his prodigious kicking feats in the 1890s, was Wisconsin's first national football celebrity. Wisconsin lore from the early years of the 20th century included such standouts as Eddie Cochems, Robert "Butts" Butler, Eddie Gillette, Cub Buck and Arlie Mucks Sr. But, the writer didn't see those stalwarts perform on the gridiron. Few people alive today did. These reminiscences feature athletes this correspondent watched in person and many of their exploits were chronicled by him during more than 37 years as a sports reporter and columnist.

McGuire is the exception. His legend was etched in the memory of a young boy who heard of his derring-do through radio accounts or saw that magic name stretched across sports pages in headlines. Henry J. McCormick, the late Wisconsin State Journal sports editor, often referred to McGuire as "Mickey Himself" after a Toonerville Folks cartoon character of that era. McGuire was christened Walter and acquired the nickname "Buster" in his native Hawaii. "Mickey" probably was the product of McCormick's imagination, or possibly that of Hank Casserly, sports editor of the Capital Times then.

The year 1932 historically is considered a time of transition. The country still was mired in the depths of the Great Depression, but Franklin D. Roosevelt defeated Herbert Hoover for the presidency that November and his campaign song, "Happy Days Are Here Again," echoed the hope a beleaguered nation sought so desperately during those trying times. Possibly McGuire and his Badger teammates captured a little of that optimism as they carved out a workmanlike 6-1-1 record that no UW team approached again for a decade. When dirty-faced youngsters in torn sweatshirts and grass-stained knickers scrimmaged in empty lots during those years, they didn't pretend to emulate Red Grange, Ernie Nevers or Bronko Nagurski. They thought of themselves as Little Mickey McGuires. He became a charismatic symbol of Badger football. Had he performed his exploits 50 years later, Mickey McGuire would have been a TV darling.

McGuire etched his name forever in Wisconsin football history by scoring all three touchdowns in the 20-13 victory over arch rival Minnesota in 1932. It climaxed a three-year career that saw him star not only in football but also as a sprinter on the track team.

He was encouraged to enroll at the university in Madison by then UW track coach Tom Jones, who saw him run with his high school half-mile relay team in the Penn Relays. That quartet held the world record for preps at the time. The kindly Jones became sort of a father image for McGuire during his years on the campus.

"My father died when I was real young," Mickey said, while describing those early years in his native Hawaii. "I wanted to go to school where nobody from the island was and work out my own problems. Nobody from my family ever had a college education and I wanted one."

He saved $300 from a job in a pineapple cannery and worked his way to San Francisco on a freighter. He came by train to Madison, rented a room for $2.50 a week and stayed for five years. There were no athletic scholarships then, so he earned money waiting on tables, teaching swimming and serving as a life guard.

"We didn't need much then," according to Dave "Moose" Tobias, one of Mickey's former teammates whose friendship with McGuire lasted a lifetime. "We wore old corduroy pants and our letter sweaters to school with no shirt. That's all we could afford."

Tobias earned money by working for Shorty Bartz, then the UW equipment man. "Thank God!" Mickey said years later. "That's the only way I got a pair of socks."

Mickey, Tobias and Frank "Moon" Molinaro, another teammate, formed an unlikely triumvirate that remained close throughout the remainder of their lives. McGuire, the Hawaiian-Irishman, Tobias, a Jew, and Molinaro of Italian ancestry met regularly through the ensuing years in Madison and these get-togethers usually occurred whenever Wisconsin renewed its rivalry with Minnesota at Camp Randall. Molinaro died in 1979 but Mickey and Dave continued their trips to Madison for visits with Moon's widow, Cappy, and the Molinaro daughters, Jill Levenhagen and Jackie Hayes.

One of those visits occurred in 1982 on the 50th anniversary of McGuire's electrifying performance against the Gophers. He had launched that victory by returning the opening kickoff 88 yards for a touchdown. There's some conjecture about how much ground he actually covered on that run. Some newspaper accounts list 88 yards and others 90. Of course, there was no instant replay then.

Tobias recalled that Badger coach Clarence "Doc" Spears grabbed McGuire by the jersey before the kickoff and exhorted him with a few choice expletives, "McGuire, you take the ball and run the slot."

"Sure enough, he ran the slot," Dave added.

Mickey scored his two other touchdowns that day on passes of 18 and 14 yards from Joe Linfor. The last one came with less than a minute to play and one newspaper story the next day related that Mickey "took the ball away from a Minnesota defenseman and fought his way the remaining three yards for a touchdown with Gophers hanging onto his legs and riding his back."

That Minnesota team, by the way, included Jack Manders, later a Chicago Bears standout, Francis "Pug" Lund of Rice Lake who left his home state to become a Gopher all-American, and a sophomore guard named Milt Bruhn, who returned to Camp Randall 17 years later as Ivan Williamson's offensive line coach.

Wisconsin lost only to Purdue that year, 7-6, and tied Ohio State at Columbus, 7-7. The Badgers missed an unbeaten season because of a botched conversion against the Boilermakers.

"I got cold-cocked in the first quarter (of the Purdue game)," McGuire recalled. "I used to hold for Joe Linfor. (Bob) Schiller replaced me and he hadn't worked with Linfor. There was a mixup and we missed the conversion."

Marquette fielded competitive football teams in those days and the Badgers beat the Hilltoppers (that was before their athletic teams became the Warriors), 7-2, in the first game that season. A game-saving tackle by McGuire on Wisconsin's 10-yard line prevented Richard Quirk from scoring a touchdown on the last play of the game. McGuire probably was the only Badger fast enough to have made that play. Quirk caught a pass from Marquette star Gene Ronzani, who later became coach of the Green Bay Packers.

Mickey made the all-Big Ten team at the conclusion of the season and his Badger teammates voted him Wisconsin's most valuable player. "I always thought Mickey and Hal Rebholz were two of the best defensive backs they ever had at Wisconsin," Tobias said of his versatile teammate.

Mickey was an outstanding punter and passer, too. One day coaches had Mickey kicking barefoot in the snow for the benefit of the press and photographers. "I went back to the house that night and soaked my feet in hot water," Mickey laughed, recalling the incident.

"Moon was a great promoter," Mickey continued. "He had a pro team and he'd pay me 100 bucks a game after our college careers. I had to play all 60 minutes and then put on a kicking exhibition barefoot at halftime. A hundred bucks was a hell of a lot of money then and I also got a free meal."

Tobias and Molinaro operated Toby and Moon's restaurant on State Street for several years after leaving school. They always said McGuire was a silent partner and promoted this with pictures of Mickey on the walls. "I never knew that until 1939," Mickey said, "so when I'd come back, that was a fun time for me. Moon would be at the counter, Dave would be cooking and I'd be at the till."

Tobias remembered that too many times during those visits Mickey would tear up the tabs of old friends who frequented the restaurant.

McGuire eventually returned to the islands after college. He served 25 years as assistant to the president of United Airlines' Pacific area. Following retirement, he became a consultant for the airlines and a director of the Hula Bowl football classic.

Although Mickey didn't always thrill to the thought of leaving his island paradise for cold blasts off Lake Mendota in November, the scent of autumn, brilliant colors on Bascom Hill and roaring crowds at Camp Randall evoked waves of nostalgia that enlivened later visits.

"My second home was always Madison," Mickey said. "People were so nice to me here."

The Fullbacks

"Weiss scored on a 40-yard run. . . he reversed his field a couple of times. . . Wisconsin fans talked about 'the run' for years afterward."

— *Tom Butler*
Author

The Great Depression of the 1930s included lean days in the University of Wisconsin football program as well. Three fullbacks — Eddie Jankowski, Howie Weiss and George Paskvan — salvaged some respectability for the beleaguered Badgers, who experienced only two winning seasons in nine years. They also finished at 4-4 a couple of times.

Following the 6-1-1 season in '32 that featured Mickey McGuire and guard Greg Kabat, Coach Clarence "Doc" Spears fell on hard times. His next three seasons produced records of 2-5-1, 4-4, 1-7 and controversy in the athletic department. Spears was ousted in a housecleaning and the athletic board hired Harry Stuhldreher, quarterback of the famed Notre Dame "Four Horsemen."

One of the off-field highlights of that era was the 1934 Homecoming celebration and return from self-exile of legendary kicker Pat O'Dea. Thousands of students and alumni crowded the Lower Campus (now the Library Mall) for a gigantic pep rally and bonfire. O'Dea, Spears and Capt. Jack Bender were among the principal speakers on the steps of the Memorial Library. The Badgers went out the next day and defeated Illinois, 7-3, to break a four-game losing streak.

The seating capacity of Camp Randall was increased from 32,700 to 35,000 in 1937 and to 45,000 in 1940. The Badgers averaged only 15,889 for five home games in 1935. That season started on an ominous note when South Dakota State came to Camp Randall and upset Wisconsin, 13-6. This was a humiliating defeat for the proud Big Ten Badgers. Fortunately, only 12,000 saw that game.

One of the keys for the Jackrabbits was stopping Jankowski, whom they managed to bottle up all afternoon. The score was tied at 6-all when Paul Miller, fleet South Dakota State left halfback, intercepted a Lynn Jordan pass and returned 62 yards for the winning touchdown.

An embarrassed Doc Spears said afterward, "It's a pretty tough beating to take but there's nothing to be done about it. Maybe it will make some of the players get down to work, but it's a shame that they wouldn't do so before they had to take a beating."

Legendary Wisconsin State Journal columnist Roundy Coughlin wrote after the game: "It don't seem possible. You've read your fairy tales and read fish stories but try and believe this. Page Winchell." (Walter Winchell was a famous gossip columnist of that day.) Fifty years later some of the South Dakota State players planned a reunion to commemorate that victory. The wife of one wrote and asked me to send all the information and clippings I could find.

Wisconsin managed only one victory in 1935 and that was another Homecoming celebration when the Badgers blanked Purdue, 8-0, in what Jankowski himself called "probably the greatest day of football I ever had in my life."

The Boilermakers came to Madison heavily favored over a team that scored only 25 points in their first five games. Purdue was led by Cecil Isbell, later a great passer with the Green Bay Packers and Jankowski's teammate there.

Jankowski dominated that Purdue game, particularly on defense, being credited with at least 20 tackles. The former Milwaukee Riverside High School star was voted most valuable player by his teammates at the end of the season.

Stuhldreher arrived the next year amid great fanfare. Notre Dame and Knute Rockne always had a great following in Madison, and Harry had been one of Rock's favorites. "The Spirit Is Back" signs proclaiming Stuhldreher's arrival were as prominent around Madison as the National Recovery Act (NRA) "We Do Our Part" insignias.

Stuhldreher brought with him the Notre Dame shift with its "swinging arms" that some likened to a chorus line. Mark Hoskins, a freshman in '39 and right halfback on the 1942 team, admitted, "Fans used to hoot when we did that (swing the arms), especially when we'd go out of town."

Not much changed on the football field in 1936 as the Badgers won only two of eight games, beating South Dakota State and Cincinnati. Ironically, Michigan and Iowa also failed to win a conference game that year. Jankowski continued as a one-man gang and received his second straight most valuable player award.

The 1937 season started with a new fullback, Weiss, and four straight victories. The Badgers shut out South Dakota State, Marquette and Chicago in succession and then beat Iowa, 13-6. They lost three of their last four games and tied Purdue, 7-7. At least the 4-3-1 mark gave Stuhldreher his first winning season and some encouragement for the next year. Continuing the fullback tradition started by Jankowski, Weiss won the first of his two most valuable player awards in '37.

The Badgers whipped Marquette and Iowa to open the '38 season but then lost for the second year in a row to Pittsburgh, 26-6. The Panthers featured the great backfield of Marshall Goldberg, Harold "Curly" Stebbins, Dick Cassiano and John Chickerneo. The university sponsored a Knot Hole Gang in those days and I still have the ticket stub from that Pittsburgh game with Goldberg's autograph on the back. The admission price for kids was 25 cents. Some of us waited outside the locker room for Goldberg to come out after the game.

Bill Daddio, an all-American end on that Pittsburgh team, later scouted for various National Football League teams and visited Camp Randall frequently. I interviewed him once and he reminisced about his days at Pitt, when the Panthers were the class of college football.

Bill Schmitz, the pride of Madison East High School, sparked the 31-13 victory over Iowa with a 67-yard scoring run from scrimmage and a 55-yard interception return for a touchdown. The latter came off Iowa star Nile Kinnick, who won the Heisman Trophy the next year.

The Badgers whipped Northwestern at Evanston, 20-13, and Weiss scored on a 40-yard run that some said clinched for him a spot on the all-American team that year. He reversed his field a couple times and Wisconsin fans talked about "the run" for years afterward.

Wisconsin also traveled west that season, scoring a 14-7 victory over UCLA and continuing Stuhldreher's program to earn national acclaim for the Badgers. He wanted to schedule opponents from coast to coast.

Wisconsin and Minnesota went into the final game of the season with identical 3-1 conference records. The winner would win the undisputed Big Ten championship. As events developed, a tie would have produced a four-way deadlock for the title with Purdue and Michigan.

The average home attendance topped 30,000 for the first time in history that season and a capacity crowd of 38,511 turned out for the Minnesota game. Wisconsin fans streamed into Camp Randall with high hopes of seeing the Badgers capture the school's first Big Ten title since 1912. However, Minnesota continued its domination, blanking the Badgers, 21-0.

The Gophers were too deep and too talented. Instead of winning or sharing the title, Wisconsin dropped all the way to fifth in the final standings with a 3-2 record.

Stuhldreher's teams always seemed to take one step forward and two back during his 13 years as head coach. Following the excitement of '38, the Badgers slipped miserably the following year to 1-6-1. They beat only Marquette, 14-13, and tied Purdue, 7-7. They lost at home to the famous Ironmen of Iowa, 19-13, with Kinnick on his way to the Heisman.

One bright spot for the Badgers was another fullback, Paskvan, the guy fans called "Roarin' George." He was a crowd-pleaser who ran with reckless abandon and tackled with fury. The LaGrange, Ill., product played only one year of high school football and that at guard. He easily adapted to fullback and led Wisconsin's offense for two straight years.

The Badgers bounced back with a 4-4 record in 1940, including 3-3 in the Big Ten. They went against mighty Minnesota in the season finale without the optimism of two years earlier. It was the 50th anniversary game in the series and the Gophers came into Camp Randall with a 7-0 record.

The largest crowd of the season — 33,557 — turned out. I watched with my dad, uncle and brother under the Field House scoreboard behind the south end zone and wondered if I was about to witness history when the Badgers jumped out to a 13-0 lead. One of Wisconsin's touchdowns came on a pass from John Tennant to sophomore end Dave Schreiner and covered 72 yards.

It wasn't to be, however. The Gophers roared back to a 22-13 victory. Once again they held too many aces with such backs as George "Sonny" Franck and Bruce Smith running behind the likes of Urban Odson, Dick Wildung and a guy with one of my all-time favorite names, Helge Pukema, a Finlander from Duluth. This Minnesota team was considered by many to be Bernie Bierman's best, and it clinched the National Championship that day.

Paskvan averaged four yards a carry and finished among the conference rushing leaders in 1939 and '40. But, he was pitted against probably the most talented running backs in the country during that era — Franck, Smith and Michigan's Tom Harmon. George still was named Wisconsin's most valuable player and all-Big Ten for the second straight year.

Wisconsin's record kept Paskvan off the all-American teams but the next August he was chosen to play in Chicago's College All-Star game and started at fullback. This just about convinced the rest of the country what Wisconsin fans knew all along, that Roarin' George was the premier college fullback in 1940.

Wisconsin's reputation for great fullbacks continued in 1941 when Marlin "Pat" Harder stormed out of Milwaukee Washington High School to become the Big Ten rushing and scoring leader, ushering in a new era for the Badgers.

Still, Wisconsin fans remembered with fondness the three fullbacks who made football a little more bearable around Camp Randall in the bleak autumns of the 1930s.

Pat Harder

"You can tie that big drum around his leg and he'll pull the drum over the goal line and 40 members of the band."

— *Roundy Coughlin*
Wisconsin State Journal

Hit 'em again, Harder! Harder! Two months before Pearl Harbor, a crewcut sophomore fullback from Milwaukee Washington High School played his first game as a Wisconsin Badger. His name was Marlin "Pat" Harder and there are those who credit him with ushering Wisconsin football into the "modern" era.

Harder became one in a long line of outstanding Wisconsin fullbacks that included Eddie Jankowski, Howie Weiss, George Paskvan, Ben Bendrick, Alan Ameche, Ralph Kurek, Alan Thompson, Ken Starch and Dave Mohapp. Many oldtimers consider Harder the best of them all.

Pat was a fullback who could run inside with power, explode on sweeps, throw option passes, catch the ball, kick field goals with deadly accuracy and spearhead the defense from his linebacker position. He epitomized the 60-minute player. Writers and broadcasters called Harder "The Mule" and "Maulin' Marlin" during that era.

The year 1941 was memorable in sports. Wisconsin won its only National Collegiate Athletic Association basketball championship. Joe DiMaggio hit safely in 56 straight games and Ted Williams compiled the last .400 average (.406) in major league baseball.

Then Harder bounded into Camp Randall and ignited a Wisconsin football resurgence that was climaxed the next year when he and Elroy Hirsch sparked the Badgers to an 8-1-1 season and a third-place ranking nationally. That team was tied by Notre Dame and beat Ohio State, losing only to Iowa, 6-0. The Helms Foundation proclaimed the Badgers national champions that year.

Years later, when Harder became a National Football League official, he often joked that he "crossed the goal line three times" at Iowa but officials never gave him a touchdown. That happened on two cracks at the Hawkeye line just before halftime. He figured he could do a better job than those officials, so he became an umpire on an NFL crew following his playing days.

World War II ended Harder's collegiate career and he enlisted in the Marines. After the war, though, he joined the NFL Chicago Cardinals as part of their "Dream Backfield" that included Paul Christman, Charley Trippi and Marshall Goldberg.

Those Cardinals won the 1947 NFL championship. Later Harder was traded to the Detroit Lions where he played on two more world championship teams in 1952 and '53. Among his accomplishments were earning all-American and all-pro honors, leading the Big Ten Conference (then the Big Nine) in rushing and scoring and being named most valuable player in the 1943 College All-Star game. He also was the Cardinals' all-time scoring leader until Jim Bakken, another ex-Badger, came along to kick for 17 years.

The sophomore season in 1941 was the only time Harder played on a losing team. The Badgers finished 3-5 that year, but Pat led the conference in scoring and rushing, including a 188-yard performance against Purdue, a remarkable feat for a two-way player. His teammates voted him most valuable player honors after the season.

It's ironic he remembers the first game (Marquette) he ever played at Wisconsin more than any other. "That was the only game I never started," he recalled years later. "I came in in the middle of the first quarter. We lost that one (28-7). I was so determined I wanted to beat those guys so bad. But the next year I threw a touchdown pass against them and that took all the sting out of it." The Badgers won that 1942 game, 35-7.

The second game in 1941 saw the Badgers lose at Northwestern, 41-14, but then they beat Iowa, 23-0, and Indiana, 27-25, in successive games at Camp Randall. Following the Hoosiers, Syracuse came to Madison with the "reverse" center and tripped the Badgers, 27-20. That's when the Syracuse center snapped the ball with his back to the defense. The ploy never caught on, however.

Wisconsin traveled to Ohio State the next week and played one of the wildest games in that long series, losing 46-34. Harder's great game against Purdue came the next week at home and then the Badgers lost at Minnesota in the season finale, 41-6, to the eventual national champions.

Harder gained 70 yards rushing in his debut against Marquette, 64 at Northwestern, 84 against Iowa, 123 against Indiana, 47 against Syracuse when injured, 74 against Ohio State while still ailing, 188 against Purdue, and 57 on 11 carries at Minnesota playing on a bad leg.

He accounted for 17 of the 23 points against Iowa with two touchdowns, a pair of conversions and a 47-yard field goal. He beat Indiana sensation Billy Hellenbrand in a running duel the next week and added 14 points. Afterward Wisconsin State Journal columnist Roundy Coughlin wrote, "Harder is the best back I've seen at Wisconsin in my time. You can tie that big drum around his leg and he'll pull the drum over the goal line and 40 members of the band. You must remember, Harder's wonderful qualifications are not all offense. It's his defense and team play. He's just one of those naturals that are hard to find."

Pat set up the first touchdown against Indiana with an end run that covered only 24 yards but ranks with the most astounding ever seen in Camp Randall. He was trapped on the sidelines by two Hoosiers but exploded through them with a burst of speed. He finally was hauled down at the Indiana seven. He scored after two plunges into the line and then kicked the conversion.

Those were difficult games. Harder was a marked man every Saturday. Opponents knew every week they had to stop him if they expected to beat Wisconsin.

"Yeah, Indiana, that was a 60-minute job going both ways," Harder recalled later. "I never got tired. The adrenalin was flowing. But, I got tired after the game. I'd go back and fall asleep. I'd have a date and had to pick the girl up at 8 o'clock and Bob Bierele, he was a track guy, would have to wake me up so I wouldn't be late."

Those 34 points Wisconsin scored at Ohio State represented the highest total for a losing team up to that time in the conference. Pat didn't play 60 minutes in that game, noting, "I got knocked silly early." He still scored two touchdowns and kicked a conversion.

He didn't play all the way at Minnesota either because of a leg injury. But, Minnesota fans always appreciated great fullbacks and they cheered Harder that afternoon. "The Minnesota fans got up and gave me a standing ovation when they took me out of the ballgame," Pat reminisced. "I scored (Wisconsin's only touchdown) and I had them hanging all over my back.

"I remember Bruce Smith and I helping each other up. We both had bad legs. (Dick) Wildung would hit me low and another guy would get me high. It wasn't all that much fun," he laughed while reflecting on that long afternoon.

Roundy, renowned for the way he fractured the king's English, wrote from Minneapolis, "Harder of Wisconsin stood out like a big toe in a little shoe. He was wonderful and Harder only had one leg. He carried three big Gophers over the goal from the 10-yard line. When you do that the

Minnesota band plays a tune for you."

Although Harder's statistics were not as impressive in 1942 as '41, he probably contributed more to the Badgers' success. He again led the team in scoring with 48 points, but an early-season injury limited his attempts from scrimmage. He gained 468 yards rushing on 116 carries. His versatility impressed everybody, though, and he made most all-American teams at fullback.

He threw a touchdown pass to Dave Schreiner, another all-American, as the Badgers beat Marquette, 35-7, and caught a scoring pass from Hirsch in the 20-19 victory at Northwestern. He wound up the season scoring five touchdowns, kicking 12 conversions and booting two field goals.

One play in the Northwestern game at Evanston exemplified Harder's importance to the Badgers. People used to accuse coach Harry Stuhldreher of being ultra-conservative, but against the Wildcats with fourth down and three yards to go on Northwestern's 41, quarterback Jack Wink sent Harder slamming into the line. Not only did Pat get the necessary yardage but he raced for a 17-yard gain. That's all the momentum the Badgers needed to continue for their second touchdown.

Harder's great blocking played a large role in Hirsch's team-leading 766 yards rushing. It was a great block by Pat that sprang Hirsch for a 59-yard run that set up a touchdown against Ohio State and another that cleared the way on Elroy's 35-yard scoring scamper against Notre Dame.

Those contributions didn't go unnoticed by Stuhldreher, who said of Pat, "His help to the other fellows was outstanding and that only goes to show that he is a fine team man."

It all happened during the early 1940s, when Friday night pep rallies were a big thing on the lower campus, football players never left the field when the ball changed sides and a guy named Marlin added pizazz to the old chant, "Hit 'em again, Harder! Harder!"

Elroy Hirsch

"Hirsch ran like a demented duck. . . his crazy legs were gyrating in six different directions all at the same time."

— *Francis Powers*
Chicago Daily News

A little more than nine months after the Japanese bombed Pearl Harbor, the University of Wisconsin began what was to become one of the school's most memorable football seasons. More than the usual excitement prevailed when practice started because everyone seemed to sense that 1942 would be the last "normal" football season for a while.

Fueling the optimism was the return of fullback Pat Harder, who led the Big Nine (Chicago withdrew from the Big Ten a couple of years earlier) in scoring and rushing the year before. Also returning was a talented supporting cast that included end Dave Schreiner, an all-American in 1941; Mark Hoskins, a two-year letterman at right halfback; and tackles Bob Baumann and Paul Hirsbrunner.

Another reason for enthusiasm was the presence on campus of a 19-year-old sophomore from Wausau named Elroy Hirsch, who enrolled at the university a year earlier with great fanfare after performing sensationally at Wausau High School. The Lumberjacks whipped Wisconsin Valley Conference opponent Merrill, 45-12, in Hirsch's final prep game and he led the way with five touchdowns on runs of 72, 42, 39, 38 and 37 yards. He also passed 30 yards for another score and had two long touchdown runs nullified by penalities.

Fans in 1941 heard stories about this freshman halfback who was running roughshod through the varsity in scrimmages that fall. When 1942 rolled around they were ecstatic at the thought of Harder and Hirsch operating in the same backfield and the two didn't disappoint them.

Three other sophomores with Hirsch — quarterback Jack Wink, center Fred Negus and right guard Ken Currier — also started that season. Evan Vogds played left guard, while Pat Lyons, Bob Hanzlik, Farnham Johnson and Hirsbrunner split left end duties. Lloyd Wasserbach took over at tackle when Hirsbrunner moved to end.

A heartbreaking 6-0 loss at Iowa prevented the 1942 Badgers from winning the conference championship and fashioning Wisconsin's first unbeaten season in 30 years. Ohio State, a team the Badgers beat, 17-7, won the title by virtue of having played one more game than Wisconsin. The Badgers also were tied, 7-7, by an outstanding Notre Dame team quarterbacked by Angelo Bertilli. Despite the one defeat and tie, Wisconsin was proclaimed national champion by the Helms Foundation in California.

Following a modest start against Camp Grant, a service team, Hirsch began to fulfill his promise with a 35-yard touchdown run in a 7-7 tie with Notre Dame. His crazy gait electrified Camp Randall fans. Hirsch didn't score against Camp Grant, but he gained 89 yards on only nine runs from scrimmage. He added 87 yards in 11 tries against the Fighting Irish.

Following the Notre Dame game, the Badgers whipped Marquette, 37 -7, and Harder avenged that 28-7 loss a year earlier in his first collegiate game. Schreiner caught three touchdown passes against Marquette, two from Wink and another from Harder on a fulback option play. Hirsch tossed a 41-yard touchdown pass to Hanzlik and scored himself on one of his patented runs that covered 20 yards. Stuhldreher watched the twisting dash by his talented sopohomore and with restrained enthusiasm that sounded more like Frank Leahy than his old coach, Knute Rockne, he called the run "a grand piece of work."

Legendary Missouri coach Don Faurot brought his Tigers to Camp Randall the next week and the Badgers earned a hard-fought 17-9 victory. Hirsch turned in probably his best performance as a Badger in this game, gaining 174 yards on 22 rushing attempts, scoring twice on runs of 19 and 7 yards and punting once for 62 yards. Harder kicked a 43-yard field goal and a conversion, while reserve fullback Bob Ray booted the other extra point. Bauman blocked a Missouri punt and a field goal attempt that helped keep the Tigers in check, while Wink and Negus came up with interceptions that snuffed out Missouri drives.

Next came the Great Lakes Navy team loaded with former college and professional stars in a ground battle at Chicago's Soldier Field. The Sailors featured Bruce Smith, the 1941 Heisman Trophy winner from Minnesota, and the one-time Windy City prep sensation Bill DeCorrevont of Northwestern as running backs. The Badgers prevailed that day, 13-7, with Hirsch scoring on an electrifying 62-yard run from scrimmage and

Wink returning a pass interception 101 yards for another touchdown that clinched the victory. Stuhldreher remembered Wink dragging himself to the sidelines after that run, dropping heavily on the bench and sighing, "I never knew 101 yards could be so long."

The Hirsch legend began to build after more of the national press watched that run at Soldier Field. There always has been some conjecture about how he acquired his nickname, arguably the most picturesque moniker in all football history. Some say Milwaukee Sentinel sports writer Stoney McGlynn was the first to call him "Crazylegs" but others credit Francis Powers of the Chicago Daily News.

"Hirsch ran like a demented duck," Powers wrote after the Wisconsin-Great Lakes game. "His crazy legs were gyrating in six different directions all at the same time" on the 62-yard touchdown run.

The Badgers blanked Purdue at West Lafayette a week later with Harder and Ray plunging for touchdowns. Pat gained 99 yards rushing on 25 carries and Hirsch 50 yards on 12 tries. It was not one of Wisconsin's most artistic performances that season. They squandered numerous scoring opportunities. The Badgers looked forward to returning home, even though the next opponent was Ohio State, like Wisconsin unbeaten.

Oct. 31, 1942, dawned crisp and clear. Poets and songwriters wax nostalgic about such autumn weather, while grid afficianados simply proclaimed the setting perfect for football. Fans streamed across Camp Randall practice fields from University Avenue and strolled down Regent and Monroe Streets in a festive mood. Although Wisconsin hadn't beaten Ohio State since 1918, optimism that bordered on cockiness pervaded the city on the eve of battle.

A crowd of 46,000, Camp Randall's capacity at that time, squeezed into the stadium. What transpired became one of the most memorable chapters in UW football history. In this magestic Homecoming setting, which was dedicated to Wisconsin men in the Armed Forces by festivities chairman Fred Rehm, a star of Wisconsin's national championship basketball team in 1941, these Badgers whipped the mighty Buckeyes convincingly.

Many side vignettes surfaced for local and national media to explore that week, such as the comparisons of fullbacks Harder and Gene Fekete, halfbacks Hirsch and Paul Sarringhaus and ends Schreiner and Bob Shaw. Also, opposing coaches Stuhldreher and Paul Brown were products of that football hotbed, Massillon, Ohio. But, football is a team game and Wisconsin proved to be the better team on this day.

Hirsch launched Wisconsin's first touchdown drive with a 59-yard run that still ranks with the most exciting ever seen in the venerable stadium. He took a direct snap from his tailback spot and headed wide around right end. Harder wiped out the first Buckeye defender with a devastating block and Hirsch leaped high to hurdle the two prone bodies. He then cut toward midfield, finally being hauled down at the Buckeye 21 on an exceptional defensive maneuver by safety Tom James, another Massillon product. Harder eventually plunged over from the two and added the extra point.

Later in the second period Harder kicked a 37-yard field goal and the Badgers took a 10-0 lead into halftime. Ohio State scored its only touchdown after a 96-yard drive early in the final quarter as Badger fans squirmed nervously in their seats. Here the Badgers demonstrated their mettle, churning 66 yards on their next possession for the clinching touchdown. Hirsch triggered the drive by returning the kickoff to Wisconsin's 34-yard line. Six plays later the Badgers found themselves with a first down on the Buckeye 14.

Harder gained 29 yards in three carries during the drive and Hirsch and Schreiner teamed for the final 14 yards with what came to be the Badgers' pet ploy that season. Hirsch started around right end but stopped suddenly, squared up and passed to a wide-open Schreiner at the goal line. Ohio State's secondary was suckered to the left, hoping to contain the explosive left halfback. Incredibly, Schreiner was ignored. Harder's conversion provided the final point in the 17-7 victory.

Wisconsin partisans huddling around radios in campus watering holes started their Homecoming revelry before the final gun even sounded. The Buckeyes needed two scores to tie or beat the Badgers, whose defense that day was beyond reproach. Statistics showed that Ohio State, with one of the country's best running attacks, was limited to four yards while trying to circle Schreiner's end position. There was a hot time in the old town that night, extending deep into the wee hours of Nov. 1.

Hirsch rolled up 118 yards on 13 rushing attempts, an average of 9.1 yards a carry. He also completed three passes. Harder gained 97 yards on 21 tries for a 4.6 average, and Schreiner caught four aerials for 54 yards while also performing impeccably on defense. If there had been video cassettes in those days, the 1942 season would have been a best-seller with Hirsch's 59-yard run against the Buckeyes the highlight.

Unfortunately the euphoria of Oct. 31 turned to total depression a week later when the Badgers traveled to Iowa and suffered through their only defeat of the season. Possibly the Badgers got caught up in the enthusiasm of their press clippings after Ohio State, or maybe it was impossible for them to achieve that emotional peak two Saturdays in a row and a letdown was inevitable. Anyway, the Hawkeyes burst the Badger bubble, 6-0. They limited Wisconsin to only 109 rushing yards, 49 by Harder and 37 by Hirsch.

Iowa scored the game's only touchdown in the second quarter but the Badgers blocked the conversion attempt. That gave Wisconsin new life. The Badgers took the ensuing kickoff and drove to the Hawkeye one.

Hirsch set up what the Badgers hoped would be the tying score with a screen pass to Harder, who bolted 14 yards to the one. Pat tried two plunges before time ran out in the half. He always insisted he crossed the goal line but the officials didn't concur. Wisconsin players and fans always wondered what might have been had he scored.

The Badgers barely got back on track the next week at Northwestern where they shaded the Wildcats, 20-19. One of the oddities of the season was that Hirsch didn't score a single touchdown in Big Nine competition. He got his chance on Wisconsin's first drive against the Wildcats but fumbled while heading for the end zone and Harder was credited with the six points when he recovered the loose ball.

The Badgers made it 14-0 in the second quarter on an 83-yard drive culminated by Hirsch's screen pass to Harder. Then, sparked by Otto Graham, an all-American who later gained fame as quarterback for the Cleveland Browns, the Wildcats rebounded with touchdowns in the second, third and fourth periods to take a 19-14 lead.

It appeared as if the Badgers might drop their second game in a row until Leonard "Bud" Seelinger, a scrappy little tailback from Great Falls, Mont., entered the picture and ignited the winning rally. Northwestern was forced to punt from deep in its own territory and the Badgers took possession on the Wildcat 36-yard line with 2 minutes left to play. This is when Seelinger came on the scene.

Bud faded to pass on first down, saw no receivers open and scrambled 21 yards to the Wildcat 15.

Harder then gained nine yards on two carries before Seelinger fired a pass to Hoskins, who dived across the goal line. It didn't matter that Harder missed the extra point because time ran out shortly afterward.

The Badgers were forced to overcome adversity many times during the season and the final game was no exception. Harder suffered a leg injury in the first preseason scrimmage and performed below par in early games, but Ray and Len Calligaro filled in admirably. The Badgers entered the finale against Minnesota without Wink, who strained leg ligaments at Northwestern, and reserve quarterback Bob Dierks, confined to the student infirmary with a severe cold.

Signal-calling responsibilities fell on the shoulders of Ashley Anderson, who carried the offensive load. Calligaro took over his defensive chores when the ball changed hands.

Wisconsin still entertained hopes for a conference title heading into the game and wasted no time proving its superiority over the Gophers. The Badgers scored what appeared to be a touchdown on their first play from scrimmage when Hirsch and Schreiner executed the halfback option pass that had been so effective all season.

The score was nullified when officials detected Dave stepped out of bounds and he was credited with only a 29-yard gain. Undaunted, the Badgers struck quickly again as Harder dashed around end for 24 yards and then bolted for five more. Hirsch then dashed to the four from where Harder scored in two plunges and followed with the conversion.

Negus set up the second touchdown by recovering a fumbled punt return at the Minnesota 32. On the first play Hirsch and Schreiner executed their favorite pass to perfection for the score and again Harder converted. The Badgers scored again on an Anderson sneak in the fourth quarter for a 20-0 lead. Minnesota finally managed a touchdown on a Bill Daley plunge late in the period but by then the Badgers were assured of their first victory over Minnesota in 10 years.

Many heroes emerged that day, including Baumann, who kept the Gophers pinned deep in their own territory with 12 booming punts on which he averaged better than 40 yards a boot. Along with those who received most of the press attention in 1942, such seniors as Pat Lyons, George Makris, Jim McFadzean, Bob McKay, John Roberts, Bob Stupka, Dick Thornally and Lloyd Wasserbach contributed to the success.

Ohio State, though, wrested the championship on the final day by beating Michigan, 21-7. Not only did the Buckeyes (5-1) win the Big Nine crown over the Badgers (4-1), they were awarded the consensus national championship as well with their 9-1 overall mark compared with Wisconsin's 8-1-1. The tie with Notre Dame undoubtedly decided the issue.

This was a disappointing conclusion for Stuhldreher, who had steered Wisconsin toward these heights for seven seasons. Making matters even worse, the Armed Forces stripped him of most of the '42 personnel before the next season rolled around. Most of them, including Hirsch, wound up as Marine officer trainees at Michigan, where they helped the Wolverines to a share of the Big Nine title in 1943. Stuhldreher coached six more years at Wisconsin but none of his later squads ever approached the caliber of the '42 outfit, and 20 years passed before Wisconsin enjoyed another eight-victory season.

Despite leading the '42 Badgers in rushing, passing, kick returns and pass interceptions, Hirsch was not always a happy camper during his brief Wisconsin career. Although it is difficult to imagine the flamboyant and charismatic UW athletic director of later years oozing anything but self-confidence, he once admitted, "At Wisconsin I was always scared. I never went into a game confident. I was never at ease playing football here. I was a sophomore on a senior-dominated team with guys like Schreiner and Hoskins. They were nice to me but the seniors hung together. We didn't mix socially. It wasn't what you'd call enjoyable football like later on. And, I was broke all the time. There were no scholarships like today. I had a job from 7 to 10 at night."

Hirsch went on to win letters in football, basketball, baseball and track at Michigan during the 1943-44 school year. He later earned National Football League immortality as a record-setting pass receiver with the Los Angeles Rams and eventually served as UW athletic director for 18 years. But, in Badger gridiron lore, he is remembered affectionately as the 19-year old sophomore who brought the Badgers national prominence with his electrifying exploits in 1942.

Touchdown Twins

"The two had been boyhood buddies. They were quintessential student-athletes and talented football players."

— *Tom Butler*
Author

When Harry Stuhldreher came to Madison in 1936, signs displayed in store windows and on back-bars around town proclaimed "The Spirit Is Back." Stuhldreher, the quarterback of Notre Dame's famed "Four Horsemen," was hired as football coach and athletic director at a divided and demoralized University of Wisconsin.

His primary job was to resuscitate the football program, which had slipped badly after fielding several good teams in the 1920s and early 1930s. He also had to mend an athletic department torn by a feud between football coach Dr. Clarence Spears and basketball mentor Dr. Walter Meanwell. The Big Ten Conference had threatened Wisconsin with expulsion unless some order replaced the chaos, and the faculty regained control of the athletic department.

Stuhldreher developed a contender in 1938, featuring all-American fullback Howie Weiss, but the Badgers experienced another one of their many disappointments by losing the championship in a 21-0 defeat at the hands of Minnesota in the final game.

Things started to perk up in 1940 and not coincidentally because two sophomores from Lancaster, Dave Schreiner and Mark Hoskins, joined the varsity. The two had been boyhood buddies. They were quintessential student-athletes and talented football players who played major roles in Wisconsin's great 1942 season.

Tragically, Schreiner lost his life fighting as a Marine Corps lieutenant on Okinawa in the closing days of World War II. Hoskins, who started at halfback for three years and piloted a B-17 in Europe during the war, later returned to his hometown to practice law. Hoskins talked about his college days during an interview in 1988 and recalled Stuhldreher "with great fondness."

"I think he was a little bit different than most of the coaches now, although he was every bit as intense. He was quite a gentleman; smart as a whip. You never heard him swear or anything like that. He was able to control his temper very well.

"One of the things I remember about him (was that) he was superstitious. I suppose that goes with the territory. He always wore the same outfit on game day. In those days coaches didn't dress uniformly. He always had on a sport coat and one of those long, wrap-around scarfs. He always wore that because one or two times he didn't wear it and we didn't come out too well."

Hoskins and Schreiner, the latter a two-time all-American end and the Big Nine's most valuable player in 1942, started as sophomores in 1940. Both scored a touchdown in their first game, a 33-19 victory over Marquette, which fielded some fine football teams in that era.

"That's when they started calling us the 'Touchdown Twins,' " Hoskins said. "It had sort of a limited application as it turned out as far as I was concerned. Or course, Dave scored many after that."

Hoskins played in the thrilling 14-13 victory at Purdue in 1940 when the Badgers scored the deciding seven points after time had run out. A huge crowd met the team at the Chicago-Northwestern depot after that victory and the Badgers received a triumphant ride in fire trucks back to the campus.

The "Touchdown Twins" later gave way to the "Three H-Boys" when Elroy Hirsch joined Hoskins and Pat Harder in the 1942 backfield. That year Hoskins scored the biggest touchdown of his career, catching a 6-yard pass from Bud Seelinger in the waning seconds to nip Northwestern, 20-19, at Evanston.

"We got up by a couple touchdowns," Hoskins recalled. "But, then Otto Graham started to limber up and put them ahead in the second half. We won it in the last 20 seconds or so.

"My place was to go out in the flat, which I did," Mark explained his winning catch. "I don't know if I was the primary receiver but (Seelinger) threw it to me. I'll never forget that."

The first two years were not easy for the twin prides of Lancaster. The Badgers compiled a 4-4 record in 1940 and were 3-5 in '41. The '42 season was a fitting climax to the careers of Hoskins and Schreiner, who had worked so diligently in previous seasons. Their teammates recognized their contributions and elected them co-captains as seniors.

"I think we were all very close," Hoskins reminisced. "When you consider '40, '41 and '42 there were some hard times over that 3-year period. We had some hard defeats. Things don't go as well when you're losing. There's no question about that. In 1942 we were winning (8-1-1) and everybody was feeling good. We had a real good mix as far as classes were concerned. Everybody got along fine."

Hoskins was part of possibly the finest backfield combination ever to perform at Wisconsin. He, Hirsch, Harder and Wink exemplified versatility. All four could pass and run, and they blocked well for each other. Hirsch and Harder, of course, became all-pro performers later and Hoskins expressed great respect for their talents.

"Pat was a do-everything guy," he said. "He could block like nobody's business and was a placekicker and a terrific runner. He was a winner.

"Elroy probably hadn't had enough time to mature yet. He was fast and had that peculiar gait and he was quite a ball-carrier. And, he really was a good blocker, too. For the first two years, when I was playing one halfback, it was awful hard to get holes opened up.

"That Notre Dame box was all single blocking; different from the single wing, where they used a lot of double blocking. Two guys would block on the tackle but we had to block man-to-man and it was hard to open up holes that way. But, I saw more open holes when I was a senior and Elroy was blocking on the other side than I did the two years before."

Schreiner was everybody's all-American following the 1942 season and the Big Ten's most valuable player. He later starred in the East-West Shrine game in San Francisco before heading into the Marine Corps. He died fighting on Okinawa in the last day of hostilities. Hoskins, a B-17 pilot flying out of Italy, was shot down over Hungary and spent almost a year as a prisoner of war. He learned of Schreiner's death just weeks after returning home in 1945. The entire state mourned Schreiner. His No. 80 jersey was retired by the UW.

"He was just exceptional," Hoskins said of his fallen friend. "He just wouldn't give up on the football field and in a lot of other things. He wouldn't take defeat. He'd just keep battling. And, he was well-liked and not conceited in any way. He was just a regular fellow."

College contemporaries remember Schreiner on "The Hill" as ruggedly handsome with cat-like grace. Moderns might scoff at the description, but Dave was the clean-cut all-American boy type, highly respected by everyone with whom he came in contact.

Stuhldreher remembered the '42 team with great affection for the rest of his life. "That outfit was close to my heart," he said long after he quit coaching. "Although not deep in reserves, that Wisconsin team was one of the finest I have ever seen. We finally licked the football bugaboo at Wisconsin and the future looked rosy. But, the war changed the whole picture.

"Hirsch was one of the best athletes I ever saw — fast, smart, dead game and hard to bring down. The greatest of all, though, was Schreiner. He had no peer at that (end) position."

Many consider the '42 team Wisconsin's greatest. If not the best, it was the one against which all succeeding teams were measured for many years afterward.

It's impossible to compare teams from different eras but the '42 squad certainly ranked with the best of its time.

"I don't think there's any question the fellows today are probably bigger and better. They just grow 'em that way now," Hoskins reflected. "But, so many people remember that ('42 team) because so many things happened. It was like a curtain dropped down. The war came along and everything was (judged) before 1942 and after 1942."

Wisconsin probably never had two such talented football players from one small community like Schreiner and Hoskins. A coach in any era would consider them a recruiter's dream.

Jug Girard

"He could make it to practice but he couldn't make it to class. . . I think he showed up in a biology lab once all semester."

— *Wray George*
Teammate

Earl Girard, nicknamed "Jug," loved fun and games. He didn't cotton to school. Attending classes at the University of Wisconsin disrupted concentration on his more serious pursuits at Camp Randall. A student-athlete he wasn't.

Girard arrived on campus in September of 1944 from his hometown of Marinette, which seemed to produce an inordinate number of talented football players. Jug might have been the best of all. He ranks with the finest all-around athletes ever to attend the UW. He excelled at every sport he tried.

Jug undoubtedly could have won nine letters, or maybe 12, had he completed his eligibility. As mentioned, he didn't like going to class. If every assistant coach and former teammate who years later claimed to have the responsibility for getting Jug to class had completed his mission successfully, Girard would be wearing a Phi Beta Kappa key today.

Following the 1944 football season, he dropped out of school and wound up in the army, returning to the campus in the fall of 1947. As an honorably discharged serviceman he was allowed to re-enroll. However, eligibility problems stalked him once more at the end of that first semester and when the 1948 season rolled around he was playing for the Green Bay Packers.

Still, his two seasons at Wisconsin were memorable. He sparked the 1944 team, comprised mostly of 17-year-olds, including himself, and played a major role during a run at the Big Nine championship in 1947. So impressive was Jug in a losing cause against a veteran Ohio State team in '44 that Bill Stern, the premier play-by-play broadcaster of that era, named him to the all-American team he selected for Look magazine that year.

The Badgers managed only a 3-6 record in 1944 but that was a marked improvement from the 1-9 of 1943, and most of the games were exciting and competitive. They lost, 20-7, to Ohio State, the eventual national champion, after going into the fourth quarter deadlocked at 7-all. They also lost at Notre Dame by 15 points, at Michigan by 14 and at home to Minnesota, 28-26.

Despite their youth these Badgers played competitively against much bigger and more mature men, many of whom were enrolled in officer training programs at schools on Wisconsin's schedule.

Girard was a non-conformist. He admits he was one of football's mavericks before it became fashionable. Jug could have kept pace with Sonny Jurgensen, and did with a former Detroit Lions teammate and one of the all-time football rounders, Bobby Layne.

"I was (a maverick)," Jug agreed in an interview long after he left Wisconsin, "but I also knew where I was going. There's nothing I would change. I enjoyed people, and thoroughly enjoyed the short time I spent in Madison. I don't think I hurt anybody in the process."

No, Jug Girard just brought a lot of pleasure and excitement to war-weary Wisconsin fans in 1944 and added to the enjoyment of several thousand veterans who crowded the campus three years later. Jug became a legend. He got fans on the edge of their seats every time he touched the ball, much like Elroy Hirsch before him and Harland Carl, Rufus Ferguson and Bill Marek, who came later.

One of Girard's 1944 teammates, Wray George, laughs when recalling Girard and some of his exploits. George was a freshman also and a graduate of Madison East High School.

"He could make it to practice but he couldn't make it to class," George recalled. "I think he showed up in a biology lab once all semester. But, Jug was a good ballplayer and he could pass. He was always good at running to his right, then jumping in the air and firing the ball. I remember all the kids who used to come over and watch practice. That's what they'd do, too — run, jump in the air and throw a pass."

"Jug could do most anything. He was a good punter, could run like the devil and was a good passer. He was a good baseball and basketball player, too. You name it. He could do it. He could have done anything in track as well as baseball or anything else. He was just a natural athlete."

Besides being young, these '44 Badgers also were small by the standards of any era. The Monday following the last game of the season Wisconsin

State Journal photographer Art Vinje took pictures of each starter on the locker room scale. The results made Bo McMillin's "po' little boys" of Indiana resemble clones of Hulk Hogan.

The heaviest was left end Jack Mead at 202 pounds. Right end Roger Laubenheimer weighed 172. Guards George and John Davey tipped the beam at 178 and 167, respectively. Tackles Martin Meyer (197) and Clarence Esser (178) dwarfed center Jack Haese at 159. Girard weighed 163, right halfback Joe Campbell 153, quarterback Nick Holmes 179 and fullback Jerry Thompson packed 160 pounds on his 5-6 frame.

Thompson was a workhorse and a tough competitor. George recalled, "Jerry and I used to argue about who was the tallest. I think we were the two shortest guys on the squad. We went both ways and I went the full 60 minutes many times," added George, who also played in 1945, '46 and '47 and later coached for many years at Columbus High School and served as athletic director there.

Following victories over Northwestern, 7-6, and Marquette, 21-2, in '44, the Badgers played their memorable game with the mighty Buckeyes at Camp Randall before 40,000, an exceptional turnout for that time. That Ohio State team included halfback Les Horvath, who won the Heisman Trophy after that season in which he led the Buckeyes to a 9-0 record.

But, Horvath wasn't the only all-American in that Ohio State lineup. Guard Bill Hackett, tackle Bill Willis and end Jack Dugger also earned that distinction in 1944, and another guard, Warren Amling, made it the next season.

Still, it was Girard who caught the attention of the national media present and inspired raves from fans leaving the stadium that day. It wasn't that his statistics threatened any records, but his flamboyant style and exceptional athletic talent kept the veteran Buckeyes on their heels most of the afternoon.

Jug's 60-minute performance included 57 yards rushing in 13 carries, four pass completions and a 37-yard average on eight punts. He also stopped one Ohio State threat with a pass interception inside Wisconsin's 10-yard line.

Girard scored Wisconsin's touchdown on a one-yard plunge and kicked the conversion. He set up the touchdown with pass completions of 37 and 17 yards. He was overshadowed by Horvath, but the eventual Heisman winner was playing his fourth collegiate season and Girard his third game.

The Buckeyes scored on their first possession and the Badgers tied the game in the third quarter. The Ohioans wore down their smaller opponents and iced the decision with two fourth-quarter scores. Only Michigan played the Buckeyes a closer game that season, losing in the finale at Columbus, 18-14.

Girard remembered the game with special pride. "The Ohio State game was the one big one because we were what we were at the time. Nothing! But, we proved something to somebody. It was the finest game as far as I'm concerned and for the whole club. It made us into a pretty good bunch of people. It put all the 17-year-olds on the map. We all matured."

George Barton, veteran Minneapolis Tribune sports writer, wrote after the Buckeye game, "Girard stamped himself one of the outstanding freshmen halfbacks of the year with his ball-carrying, passing, punting and defensive play.

"The spectators were tense with excitement every time Jug took the ball, for there was no telling when he might shake loose for a touchdown sprint or complete a pass to Ed Bahlow or Jack Mead for a score.

"Jug's brilliant work in all departments and the ferocious way his teammates collaborated with him in a desperate effort to turn defeat into victory kept the battle interesting until the final period when Ohio's power again asserted itself and netted the Buckeyes two more touchdowns."

Girard was the epitome of the triple-threat halfback. He ran, passed, punted and even place-kicked points after touchdown. His conversion beat Northwestern, 7-6, in the opening game. Two of Jug's passes at Northwestern went for apparent touchdowns of 48 and 39 yards, but they were nullified by penalties. He also averaged 46.1 yards on eight punts.

The next week he connected with Mead for scores of 25 and 5 yards in a 21-2 victory over Marquette. He had another apparent passing touchdown against Marquette wiped out by an infraction. Thompson led Wisconsin ground-gainers agaist Marquette with 103 yards in 14 attempts while Girard contributed 80 yards in 23 carries.

A week after the Ohio State game the Badgers bowed at Notre Dame, 28-13, but Girard passed 13 yards to Mead for one touchdown and kicked the conversion.

Losses to Great Lakes and Purdue followed and Girard was relieved for the first time that season against the Sailors after playing 60 minutes the first four games. He also injured a knee at Purdue and didn't play against Iowa, a 26-7 victim of the Badgers, and at Michigan, where they lost, 14-0. Tragedy struck in the Iowa game when UW quarterback Allen Shafer was injured in the second half and died shortly afterward in the hospital. His shaken teammates were mostly ineffective the following week at Michigan.

The season ended with a heartbreaking 28-26 loss to Minnesota at Camp Randall. Girard was rusty from sitting out two straight games and missed on his first eight passes. He regained his earlier form as the game progressed, passing for one touchdown, running for another and setting up a third with his throwing. He hit Mead for a 23-yard score and finished with seven completions for 159 yards. He added 46 yards on 15 runs from scrimmage.

When Girard returned in 1947 he found a squad much more mature and talented than the one in '44. Halfbacks Gene Evans, Clarence Self, Earl Maves and Gwynn Christianson as well as fullback Ben Bendrick, end Bob Rennebohm and center Robert "Red" Wilson were just a few of the standouts Stuhldreher had assembled that season.

A 48-7 lacing at the hands of a powerful California team and a 7-7 tie at Indiana were the only blemishes on Wisconsin's record after the first seven games. The Badgers whipped Purdue, 32-14; Yale, 9-0; Marquette, 35-12; Northwestern, 29-0, at Evanston; and Iowa, 46-14, at Camp Randall. They came into a showdown at home against unbeaten Michigan with a chance to take the Big Nine lead with an upset of the mighty Wolverines.

Unfotrtunately for the Badgers, that was the last and probably the greatest of all coach Fritz Crisler's Michigan teams. It featured Bob Chappuis, Bump and Pete Elliott, Howard Yerges, Jack Weisenburger and Alvin Wistert. The Wolverines executed Crisler's intricate offense with its spinning fullback to perfection. Today they still are considered among college football's greatest teams.

When the teams arrived at Camp Randall that Nov. 15, they found the field soggy from slushy snow that fell on the city during the early morning hours. Wisconsin fans thought possibly the weather "fates" had dealt them an ace because the Michigan offense, which depended so much on sleight-of-hand, would be susceptible to fumbles on the wet field. As events developed, the Wolverines didn't miss a beat all afternoon as they trounced the Badgers, 40-6.

The Badgers never recovered from the shock and also lost the next week at Minnesota, 21-0. Michigan completed its unbeaten season with a 21-0 victory over Ohio State and a resounding 49-0 trouncing of Southern California in the Rose Bowl.

Despite losing those last two games, Wisconsin finished second in the conference and Badger fans recall many highlights from that season. Ranked high among those performances were Girard's running and passing that helped beat a strong Northwestern team, 29-0, and Jug's punt returns of 63 and 85 yards for touchdowns in the first quarter that launched the 46-14 victory over Iowa.

Red Wilson, Wisconsin's most valuable player that season, just as he was in '48 and '49, remembered Girard as a "likeable" guy who just lacked direction while a student at Wisconsin.

"Girard was, in my opinion, maligned as a personality because he was such a character," Wilson said. "It wasn't that he was such a wild and unpredictable person. It was just that he was not prepared to do some things that the ordinary guy would do, knowing that if he didn't do them, he wouldn't be able to play football anymore. That didn't seem to bother him.

"But, he was very pleasant, very likeable and very business-like on the football field. Plus, he was a terrific athlete. He was well-liked and never caused any problems for anybody except he didn't go to class. It wasn't that he overslept or anything like that. He just didn't care to go to school.

"It's too bad the right person didn't get hold of him, sit him down and said, 'Hey, this is something that's really going to be valuable to you as you go through life and it's the thing to do.'

"He wasn't stupid. In fact, I think he was a reasonably bright guy, the way he talked, the way he carried himself socially and stuff like that. He wasn't really a bad actor. He just didn't go to class."

Besides spending a couple years with the Packers, Jug played on two championship teams at Detroit and closed out his career with the Pittsburgh Steelers.

Also, early in his career, playing for the Green Bay baseball franchise, Girard won the 1950 batting championship in the old Class D Wisconsin State League with a .367 average. He hit 19 doubles, nine triples and six homers while driving in 91 runs. He also starred as a semi-pro basketball player. Wilson was right. Anybody who performed effectively in so many sports had to be sharp mentally as well as physically.

Years after that '44 season, Jug could recall events vividly. "I remember almost everything. I've gone over some clippings, going over all the faces and names, wondering where they are and, I hope, vice versa. They were a wonderful bunch of people. I remember just the days and weeks on the field. For me to come in as a young punk and be accepted. I think we did a hell of a job, a lot more than anyone expected we could do. We had unity and everyone enjoyed it."

Anybody around Camp Randall during the '44 and '47 seasons never forgot the guy called Jug either.

Robert Wilson

"Wilson's feat of being voted most valuable football player three straight years is unprecedented in the history of the sport at the UW."

— *Tom Butler*
Author

Robert "Red" Wilson once was described as "a big center with hands like hams and a conviction that football to be enjoyable should be strictly robust."

That description came from the typewriter of Henry J. McCormick, former Wisconsin State Journal sports editor, following the Shrine High School All-Star football game in 1946. Wilson and Lisle Blackbourn Jr., both Milwaukee Washington graduates, sparked the South team, coached by Lisle Blackbourn Sr., to a 20-7 victory over the North. The younger Blackbourn scored two touchdowns and Wilson provided fans with a "robust" performance they came to expect from him for the next four seasons in Wisconsin's cardinal and white. Blackbourn also starred for the Badgers during those years.

Not only did Wilson sparkle on the gridiron, but also as a baseball catcher for the Badgers under coach Arthur "Dynie" Mansfield and later as a major leaguer for 10 years with the Chicago White Sox and Detroit Tigers.

Wilson's feat of being voted Badger most valuable football player three straight years is unprecedented in the history of the sport at the UW. He played center and linebacker when his teammates honored him as a sophomore in 1947 and a junior in '48. He was switched to end as a senior under new coach Ivan Williamson in '49 and not only repeated as Badger MVP, but also received the Chicago Tribune trophy as the Big

Ten's most valuable player.

Wilson experienced the tumultuous transition from Harry Stuhldreher to Williamson following the '48 season. It wasn't a pleasant experience and Red had mixed emotions over the switch.

Following Wisconsin's abortive run for the championship in '47, the Badgers fell on hard times in '48 when their record slumped to 2-7. The season provided little enjoyment for the Badgers or their fans. Stuhldreher had lost touch with the "modern" game and raised the ire of fans because of his "unimaginative" offense. The disenchantment led to the infamous "Goodbye Harry" signs and Stuhldreher's eventual departure as coach, although he did remain as athletic director for two more years.

Wilson admitted Stuhldreher's system was "a little behind the times." The Badgers operated out of the old Notre Dame box but they also did run some from the T-formation.

"I recall in '47 we played Northwestern and used the open huddle," Red said. "We'd come up to the line and Northwestern would be in one defense and we'd run a reverse. If they were in another defense, we'd run a fake reverse with a trap up the middle. Well, we just killed 'em (29-0).

"Then when we came up to play Michigan (for first place), somehow, maybe it wasn't all that difficult, but they knew the basic system of calling plays. The plays were called in three 2-digit numbers, like '22, 46, 58, hike.' If it was 22, the 2 would dictate which direction we were going; 23 would be going to the other side.

"So, basically they knew our offense; not all the details, but what really worked against Michigan were the reverse plays because the play would start out 22 but then the rest of the digits would indicate it was a reverse.

"At any rate you just felt they knew where our plays were going because at that time I was centering and all I could see would be the heels of the guy over the center going one way or the other, depending on which way the play was called. The only plays that really confused them were the reverse plays. The only score we made was on a reverse that Jim Embach carried."

Wilson figures the seeds of Stuhldreher's troubles were sewn during those last two games of '47 when the Badgers fell out of the Big Nine race by losing to Michigan and Minnesota. Still, there were high aspirations for '48 despite the loss of some key people, including Jug Girard, Earl Maves, Bob Rennebohm and Jack Wink.

The Badgers played Indiana at Camp Randall in the first game that season and the George Taliaferro-led Hoosiers whipped them, 35-7. The following week they shaded Illinois at home, 20-16, for their only conference win of the season. Next came California at Berkeley and a 40-14 trouncing. Then they returned to Madison and lost to Yale, 17-7. "We stunk up the place," Wilson said of the Yale game.

"Goodbye Harry" signs started to appear around campus and the Badgers were happy to head for Columbus the next week where they played Ohio State tough but lost a heartbreaker, 34-32. "We really pushed Ohio State all over the field but we didn't have a pass defense," Red lamented. "Gene Evans had a hell of a day."

The Badgers also lost three of their final four games, beating only Marquette, 26-0. The situation got pretty ugly before the season ended with a 16-0 loss to Minnesota in the finale at Camp Randall. Stuhldreher's fate was sealed.

Most of the coach's players felt badly about the adverse treatment directed toward him, but they were ready for a change, too. Wilson pointed out that Stuhldreher had one full-time coach. The rest of the staff also taught in the physical education school. He also was burdened with the added responsibilities of athletic director.

"It was really tough," Wilson said of the '48 season. "Harry was a real gentleman and a very compassionate and caring individual for his players. He did everything he could to encourage us, but the ball started rolling downhill and we obviously had some shortcomings."

A similarity of names caused some confusion when Ivan Williamson was hired to succeed Stuhldreher as coach because Wisconsin also had been interviewing Bud Wilkinson of Oklahoma. Williamson, a virtual unknown as far as Badger fans were concerned, brought his staff from Lafayette College and the group concentrated exclusively on football, unlike the part-time nature of most Stuhldreher assistants.

"So, the level of professionalism and staff support to the football program was substantially greater when Williamson came in," Wilson said. "A majority of the staff was full time and Ivy wasn't involved in being athletic director. Plus, he was a hell of a bright guy and a hell of a good coach."

Williamson changed the direction and perception of Wisconsin football from the day his Badgers stepped on the field for their first game against Marquette in 1949 and whipped the Hilltoppers, 41-0. The Badgers went from a 2-7 team in '48 to a 5-3-1 outfit that challenged for the championship right up to the final game.

Wilson recalled an incident in that first game against Marquette that set the tone for the next six years. "The play that really created the fan turnaround was a fake field goal that we scored a touchdown on," he said. "I think the fans thought, 'Hey, this is something we've been looking for for a long time.' You know how fans are!"

One of the most significant aspects of the 1949 season was the conversion of Wilson from a center and linebacker to an offensive end and linebacker. Red always played linebacker but as a high school sophomore he was stationed at guard. His prep coach, Liz Blackbourn, later a Badger assistant and Green Bay Packer head coach, switched him to center as a senior.

"It was Ivy's idea," Wilson said of his move to end. "In his offense he wanted somebody bigger and a better blocker (at end). The way he used me was like a tight end. I could run reasonably well, had reasonably good hands and was a good blocker."

Joe Kelly took over at center and Wilson shared time at end with Tilden Meyers, who played end in high school and could run a little faster than Red. But, Williamson's offense stressed the blocking tight end and that's where Wilson excelled, and he also demonstrated he could catch the football.

"I had some concerns about it (the move to end) in a selfish sense," Red admitted. "I felt, gee, I've been a center for three years and developed something of a reputation at that position. From a standpoint of recognition, I felt selfishly this isn't such a good idea.

"But, on the other hand, I thought, this is kind of neat. It's going to be an interesting challenge. I'll get a chance to catch the ball and do some different things. I enjoyed it very much. It provided a new challenge and created a lot more interest for me as a senior.

"And, it was a very significant factor in my being elected Big Ten most valuable player. People said, 'Here's a guy who went to another position and helped out the team.' And, it really was fun."

Bob Petruska, the pride of Lake Mills, took command at quarterback that season, while halfbacks Bob Teague, Gene Evans, Jim Embach, Lisle Blackbourn and Gwynn Christensen provided some excitement with their running behind one of the finest lines ever to represent Wisconsin. It featured Wilson, Ken Sachtjen, Kelly, Bill Gable, Don Knauff, Hal Otterback and Ken Huxhold.

Following the victory over Marquette that season, the Badgers battled Illinois to a 13-all tie, lost to California, 35-20, and bounced back to trim Navy, 48-13. Then old nemesis Ohio State blanked them at Camp Randall, 21-0, as a harbinger of things to come from the Buckeyes during Williamson's tenure.

However, the Badgers leaped back into championship contention with successive victories over Indiana, 30-14, Northwestern, 14-6, and Iowa, 35-13. The Badgers had a shot at sharing the championship with Ohio State and Michigan heading into the final game at Minneapolis but Minnesota prevailed, 14-6, featuring such Gopher immortals as Bud Grant, Clayton Tonnemaker, Leo Nomellini and Gordy Soltau.

Williamson's seven years produced a 41-19-4 record, including 29-13-4 in the Big Ten. The Badgers' only championship was a tie with Purdue in 1952 but they could have figured in six straight titles with one more victory in each of the five other seasons. His 1955 team slumped to 4-5 and he took the reins of athletic director in December, succeeding Guy Sundt, who died in October that year. Milt Bruhn, Williamson's able line coach, took over the football program.

Ivan's first season, though, set the tone for Wisconsin's most productive stretch since the turn of the century. Wilson's performance on the field and his senior leadership as captain played major roles in getting Williamson's tenure off on a positive note. When Red's baseball career ended, he returned to Madison and became a bank executive, while continuing his close association with the university and its athletic program.

The Hard Rocks

"Injuries on defense? Hell, no! . . . 'Football is a hitting game. If you don't like to get hit, get the hell out of there.' "

— *Pat O'Donahue*
Defensive End

Wisconsin football fans remember them as the "Hard Rocks." Pat O'Donahue affectionately called his old teammates "a bunch of renegades." The late Ivan Williamson often said that it was the best team he ever coached.

Seldom does a defensive unit in college football earn a special nickname of its own, but the 1951 Badgers were so honored. This bunch led the nation in defense, allowing only 601 yards rushing in nine games. They compiled a 7-1-1 record, their only blemishes being a 14-10 loss at Illinois and a 6-6 tie with Ohio State. The loss cost them the Big Ten Conference title, won by the Illini with a 5-0-1 mark.

"That's still the best football team this school ever had," O'Donahue, an all-American defensive end in 1951, said during a 1981 interview. When the reporter to whom he made that statement conceded his claim might be true, O'Donahue thundered, "Might be! That's the truest statement you'll ever hear."

Everything is relative, but 'ol Pat just might be right. Those '51 Badgers did everything but go unbeaten and win the Big Ten championship. They led the conference in rushing, passing, scoring and, of course, defense. Yet they finished third behind Illinois and Purdue (4-1). The Badgers compiled a 5-1-1- mark in the conference.

Minneapolis Tribune writer Charley Johnson called those Badgers the best Big Ten football team ever to finish third. They were 1-1-1 after the first three games and undefeated the rest of the way. Following an opening 22-6 victory over Marquette came the loss at Illinois and the Ohio State deadlock.

Then those Badgers whipped Purdue, 31-7 at Lafayette, Ind.; Northwestern, 41-0 at Evanston, Ill.; Indiana, 6-0 in the famous Camp Randall "Snow Bowl;" Pennsylvania, 16-7, and Iowa, 34-7, at home; and Minnesota, 30-6, in Minneapolis.

The loss at Illinois was a bitter defeat. The Badgers led the Illini in first downs (20-8), yards rushing (136-85) and passing (164-113), but some controversial penalities killed Wisconsin's chances that day. O'Donahue recalled Wisconsin leading, 10-7, with a first-and-goal at the Illinois two-yard line.

"Then the official called two penalties right in a row. You should see the film. He had his hand on the handkerchief before the ball was snapped," O'Donahue insisted.

"He called our guard pulling and the play didn't even call for our guard to pull, and he didn't pull. He called a guy in motion on the next play and we were going backwards. We never did score. It would have been 17-7 and it would have been all over."

The usual defensive lineup for the Badgers that year included ends O'Donahue and Gene Felker or Don Voss, tackles Jerry Smith and Bob Leu, nose guard Bob Kennedy, linebackers Hal Faverty, Deral Teteak and Roger Dornburg, cornerbacks Eddie Withers and Jim Hammond and safety Bill Lane.

Felker started out playing on offense and defense, but an injury curtailed his activity midway through the season. Voss got his chance when freshmen became eligible beause of the Korean War. The next year he made all-American.

This was essentially a homegrown lineup. Smith came from Dayton, Ohio; Faverty from Evanston, Ill.; and Dornburg from Naperville, Ill. But O'Donahue hailed from Eau Claire, Kennedy from Rhinelander, Leu from Ripon, Voss and Felker from Milwaukee, Teteak from Oshkosh, Withers from Madison, Hammond from Appleton and Lane from Edgerton.

Senior quarterback John Coatta directed the offense, led the Big Ten in passing and had one of the most crafty football minds ever to guide a Badger offense. That also was the year Alan Ameche of Kenosha stormed onto the football scene as a freshman fullback and set a Big Ten rushing record. Rollie Strehlow played left halfback because Harland Carl of Greenwood was injured most of that season. Jerry Witt of Marshfield became a great spot player at right halfback and led the Big Ten in scoring and pass receiving.

The defense was made up mostly of seniors except for Voss, Kennedy and Dornburg. That unit remained reasonably free of injuries and when one player was hurt, a more than adequate replacement always seemed to emerge.

"Injuries on defense? Hell, no!" O'Donahue exclaimed. "We didn't get hurt. Ivan used to teach us one thing: 'Football is a hitting game. If you don't like to get hit, get the hell out of here. You do the hitting.' "

Hammond captained the '51 team. Faverty was voted most valuable player and received all-American recognition along with O'Donahue and Withers. Coatta earned all-Big Ten honors and just about everybody from the defensive unit received all-conference recognition from one source or another.

Defensively, the "Hard Rocks" dominated everybody. The defense alone outscored all opponents, 58-53, with four touchdowns — two on pass interceptions and two on fumble recoveries in the end zone — plus four safeties. Conversions and field goals accounted for 26 points because nine of the 11 defensive players also lined up on the kicking unit.

"The 1951 team was the strongest of any I coached," Williamson once reflected after he retired from the field and became Wisconsin athletic director.

A 16-7 non-conference victory over Pennsylvania exemplified the "Hard Rocks" because the defense accounted for all 16 points. Teteak recovered a bad snap in the end zone and Leu ran back an interception for touchdowns and O'Donahue tackled a runner in the end zone for a safety.

Teteak, who credited former Wisconsin State Journal sports editor Henry J. McCormick for the "Hard Rocks" nickname, summed up the defense this way: "I think we just had some pretty good players and I think everybody believed in the other guy; that he was going to do his job and you were going to do yours no matter what.

"And, Ivan did a good job. We had all kinds of defenses — do this and do that. Then we'd get in the ball game and use one defense. We didn't need more apparently. We used the same old straight 5-3-3 and just stayed with it."

Laughing as he recalled his touchdown against Penn, Teteak said, "That was funnier than hell. In the old days we got paid so much for a touchdown. I can remember knocking Smitty out of the way and knocking O'Donahue out of the way and knocking a couple other guys out of the way to get to the ball."

O'Donahue said, "Penn was a big one because the year before Penn beat us out in the City of Brotherly Love. They humiliated us. We pointed for that game probably more than any of our conference games because we were a wee bit smitten. We kicked hell out of them and they broke off relations after that game.

"We set a record for penalties (10 for 130 yards). I don't know, it still might be a record. It was a vicious game. It wasn't what you'd call a masterpiece for sportsmanship or anything else. We kicked hell out of 'em to make up for the year before."

Not only did the '51 Badgers dominate everybody defensively, they stood head and shoulders above their conference rivals on offense, scoring 158 points compared with the second-best total of 116 by Purdue. Coatta became the first Big Ten player to pass for more than 1,000 yards in a season and he set a conference accuracy record of .642, completing 52 of 81 attempts. Ameche established a Big Ten rushing record with 774 yards in seven games and Witt led the league in pass receiving and scoring.

Those Badgers launched the '51 season with a 22-6 victory over Marquette. The defense provided a harbinger of things to come that season when Smith blocked a Hilltopper punt, the ball rolling out of the end zone for a safety, and Dornburg returned a pass interception for a touchdown.

Then the offense took over as Carl raced 81 yards to set up Strehlow's short touchdown run, and Hammond broke free for 40 yards that led to another Strehlow score. One particularly significant incident occurred when a freshman named Ameche replaced sophomore fullback Bob Lamphere and gained one yard on the final play of the game. Three years later he was awarded the Heisman Trophy.

Illinois great Johnny Karras scored both Illini touchdowns in the long-lamented 14-10 loss in the second game. Hammond pounced on a Karras fumble in the end zone for Wisconsin's touchdown as the defense continued earning its legendary reputation. Coatta kicked the conversion and a 24-yard field goal to round out Badger scoring. The Badger offense roared up and down the field that day but couldn't put the ball in the end zone and this inability to culminate these drives successfully cost Wisconsin its first unbeaten season and conference championship since 1912.

The Badgers returned to Camp Randall for their third game against Ohio State, which featured 1950 Heisman Trophy winner Vic Janowicz. The Badgers scored first with 1:02 left in the first half on a six-yard pass from Coatta to Faverty. Later Ameche, who gained 79 yards rushing that day and began to pop some eyes around the conference, spearheaded a drive that resulted in Coatta missing a 20-yard field goal attempt.

That didn't seem to matter because the defense was keeping the Buckeyes in check. Finally, though, Hammond punted 46 yards and the visitors set up a reverse that completely fooled the Badgers, enabling Bernie Skavarka's return to Wisconsin's five-yard line. After gaining one yard on two plunges, Janowicz passed to Ralph Armstrong for the touchdown. The extra point attempt sailed wide and the game ended in a frustrating stalemate.

This, however, ended frustrations for 1951. The Badgers regrouped after the 6-6 tie and stormed past their next six opponents, starting with a

31-7 victory at Purdue. Ameche fashioned his first 100-yard game (148) against the Boilermakers and scored his first collegiate touchdown on a seven-yard burst. The Badgers made it 9-0 on a safety when Voss blocked a Purdue punt out of the end zone. Coatta threw touchdown passes of 47 yards to Witt and 14 yards to Strehlow. The Badgers got another safety and Ameche rambled 64 yards to the Purdue one, setting up Witt's scoring run.

The next Saturday at Northwestern before 50,000 fans and countless others watching on television the Badgers probably reached their peak while registering a 41-0 victory. Witt enjoyed a career afternoon, scoring four touchdowns — two on passes covering 16 and 60 yards, and two more on runs for four and 60 yards from scrimmage.

Burt Hable, long-time coach at Madison West High School who played quarterback and defensive back, hit Kent Peters with a short touchdown pass to boost the Badgers in front, 35-0, late in the third quarter. Reserve halfback Bill Schleisner scored the final touchdown on a short run in the final period. The conversion failed and that was about the only mistake the Badgers made all day.

The "Hard Rocks" limited the Wildcats to 23 yards rushing and 90 passing in the shutout. Ameche took advantage of his first collegiate start by recording his second straight 100-yard game as the offense accounted for 572 yards, 371 on the ground and 201 through the air. Witt accounted for 233 yards and four touchdowns in just over two quarters of action, while Ameche added 124 yards and Coatta threw for 166 yards and two touchdowns.

Wisconsin returned home the next Saturday to gain its second straight shutout, 6-0, in the snow against Indiana.

The temperature dipped to 20 degrees at kickoff and a 25-mile-per-hour wind out of the southeast carried snow that measured 9 inches in the city before the flakes subsided late in the afternoon. One remarkable aspect of the game was that 50,000 of the 51,000 who bought tickets showed up, many arriving early in the second quarter after battling traffic snarls caused by the snow.

Wisconsin outgained the Hoosiers, 267 total yards to 91, and dominated the action but fumbled 10 times, losing five. It seemed as if the game would end in a disappointing scoreless tie. Indiana fumbled only three times and lost one, but that lone turnover paved the way for Wisconsin's victory.

Lane recovered Hoosier Jerry Ellis' fumble at the Indiana 35 with little more than a minute left. Moments later Coatta hit Billy Hutchinson with a pass in the end zone with 58 seconds on the clock. It made no difference that the extra point attempt failed.

Ameche gained 57 yards in the first half but had trouble hanging onto the ball and didn't play after intermission. Hammond took over and gained 86 yards, while Strehlow added 81 and Witt 63.

Next the Badgers beat Pennsylvania and Iowa at home. After yielding only 13 yards rushing to Penn, the "Hard Rocks" girded for the Hawkeyes, who featured Bill Reichardt, the Big Ten's leading rusher at the time. The Badger defense stymied Reichardt, who managed only 13 yards in 11 carries, while Ameche rolled up 126. Coatta passed for 119 yards, including a scoring shot to Strehlow that covered 53 yards as the Badgers won handily, 34-7.

Witt scored twice and Ameche once. Carl, who languished on the sidelines most of the season because of injuries, returned to action and sparked the final touchdown drive. He carried the ball three times for 30 yards and caught two passes from Hable, the last covering 12 yards for the score.

The final game at Minnesota belonged to Ameche, who capped his freshman season with 200 yards rushing and two touchdowns. His 774 yards in seven Big Ten games broke the conference record. Faverty ran for the third touchdown. Coatta kicked a 17-yard field goal in the third quarter and scored on a quarterback keeper from eight yards out in the final period.

O'Donahue said Wisconsin assistant coach George Lanphear recruited most of the 1951 team and they remained a close-knit group. For instance, he, Felker, Faverty, Coatta, Teteak and Smith lived together all four years, sharing an apartment on State Street the last three.

"We joined forces and stayed together," O'Donahue said. "We've all been pretty close ever since. We keep track of each other anyway. That was the difference with that ballclub.

"I'll tell you how goofy they were. Jerry Smith had a room around the corner from Brown's Book Store and he never stayed there. He slept on the davenport in our apartment for two years. He paid rent down at the other place and never went in it. That's how close we were."

Pat also remembered Fred Marsh, one of Williamson's longtime assistants, once telling him, "Ivan made one statement on the way home from the Minnesota game. He said to his assistants, 'You fellows probably will never realize what a great team you coached this year.'

"You look up Ameche's record," O'Donahue added, "and you'll see his average per carry was the best as a freshman of his four years. But, he had a helluva quarterback (Coatta) directing him, too.

"They were a hell of a motley crew," Pat mused with obvious affection. "They're a bunch of renegades. You'd have to know 'em to appreciate 'em."

Wisconsin fans haven't known the likes of the "Hard Rocks" since and chances are they never will again.

"The Horse"

"You had to key your defense for him or he'd run away with you, He was just overpowering. He was a terrific athlete."

— *Gary Messner*
Center

Wisconsin rode " The Horse"' on its most successful football run in the 20th century. Alan Dante Ameche was the catalyst of coach Ivan Williamson's Badger resurgence in the 1950s and the Kenosha native became the most celebrated of all UW grid heroes.

A powerful fullback nicknamed "The Horse"' by assistant coach George Lanphear, Ameche earned all-American honors twice and became the school's only Heisman Trophy winner in 1954. His success and popularity attracted outstanding young athletes to the university for a decade after he graduated.

Ameche matriculated at Wisconsin following a brilliant career at Kenosha Bradford High School. He tore up Illinois in a junior varsity game behind the stadium early in the 1951 season and Williamson quickly promoted him to the varsity where he became an immediate star.

Lanphear always claimed he named Ameche "The Horse" because the rugged fullback worked like a horse in practice. However, he might have picked up the moniker from his unusual gait, too, running with knees high and arms flailing.

A halfback in high school, Ameche easily adapted to fullback. He set a Big Ten rushing record as a freshman, earned all-American honors as a junior and senior and was named to the school's all-time team ahead of several other great fullbacks.

Ameche, who died unexpectedly Aug. 8, 1988, following a heart attack at the age of 55, returned to Madison for the Northwestern game in 1984 and at halftime presented his Heisman Trophy to then athletic director Elroy Hirsch as a gift to the university which he said had given him so much.

"It was the appreciation and the love, I guess you'd say, I have for the school and I guess that's gotten stronger, too, as the years have worn on, " Ameche said then. "I think I went through a period, when I was younger, when I felt almost like the school owed me. Now, as I reflect back and when you get more mature you realize how much the school really did for you."

Ameche played 37 games at Wisconsin, including the 1953 Rose Bowl. He appeared only three minutes against Illinois as a senior because of an injury, but most of the time he was there whenever Williamson and the Badgers needed him.

Wisconsin compiled a 26-8-3 record, 18-5-3 in the Big Ten, during Ameche's four years. The Badgers and Purdue tied for the Big Ten championship in 1952, the school's first title in 40 years. Wisconsin's overall record that year of 6-2-1, compared with Purdue's 4-3-2, earned the Badgers a Rose Bowl bid. The two teams did not meet that season. That was their only championship during Ameche's career. Ironically, had the Badgers scored one more victory in each of those four seasons, they could have figured in four straight championships.

Usually Ohio State was the culprit. Those two teams tied, 6-6, in 1951, Ameche's freshman season, and the Buckeyes then chalked up three straight victories by scores of 23-14, 20-19 and 31-14. If the Badgers had beaten Illinois in '51 and Ohio State the next three years, they would have come away with three undisputed titles and a share of the crown with the Buckeyes in '54.

Although the Badgers can point to some impressive victories in 1952, during an interview in 1984 Ameche said the Illinois game of 1953 stood above all the rest in his memory. The Illini, with J.C. Caroline and Mickey Bates, came to Madison unbeaten in seven games.

Illinois marched for a touchdown in its first possession and it seemed on that sunny, crisp autumn Saturday the Illini would notch another victory with little difficulty. As the game progressed, though, that was the extent of their scoring. The Badgers trounced them, 34-7, with Ameche gaining 145 yards in 17 carries.

"It really came down to quite a showdown and we just pushed them all over the place," Ameche said. "I really felt good about that one."

Legendary sports writer Red Smith came from New York to witness the confrontation between the two Big Ten powers, particularly the Ameche-Caroline matchup, and he wrote after the game, "Illinois stopped at the sign of the Flying Red Horse," paraphrasing a prominent oil company promotion of that era.

"There were a lot of exciting moments," Ameche continued. "The Rose Bowl unfortunately lives in my mind even to this day as an infamous situation. But, it was a big game, no question about it."

The Badgers lost the '53 Rose Bowl to Southern California, 7-0, but Ameche gained 133 yards on 28 rushing attempts, including one run of 54 yards.

"I took a pitchout on the first play of the second half and the blocking was perfect," Ameche reminisced more than 30 years later. "It was just a question of going all the way. I could have made it an 80-yard run but I got caught from behind.

"Then they stopped us. We didn't even get a field goal out of it. But, that's one of those things that haunt you. If I'd have had the O.J. Simpson or Jim Brown kind of speed, I'd have been in the end zone, no question about it. But, you do the best with what God gave you.

"I had a good burst. I had a good start and I hit the line well and could cut well. But, I didn't have that kind of speed to outdistance those quick safeties. They always seemed to catch me."

"The Horse" was too tough on himself. He had at least seven runs better than 40 yards during his career and many of his shorter romps came in clutch situations. His 24-yard touchdown gallop on a wet, slippery field beat Marquette, 13-11, in 1953 and his 29-yard run the next year enabled Wisconsin to nip Michigan State, 6-0, at East Lansing.

Ironically, he made history by running 79 yards for a touchdown against the Chicago Bears on his first carry as a pro in 1955. "It was the first time I even touched the ball (in the pros)," he said. "I never even came close to that again. I did have a few fairly long touchdown runs but nothing close to that (in high school, college or the National Football League)."

It was Ameche's one-yard touchdown plunge in sudden death overtime that enabled the Baltimore Colts to beat the New York Giants, 23-17, for the 1958 NFL title in what often is called the "greatest game of all-time." His touchdown has been shown on television hundreds of times since, even to this day.

"That was probably the shortest run I ever made and the most remembered," he reflected.

When Ameche left Wisconsin, he owned National Collegiate Athletic Association four-year career records for rushing attempts (673) and net yards (3,212). He went on to play six years for the Colts, including the 1958 and '59 championship teams.

Besides being named all-Big Ten three times and all-American twice, "The Horse" was awarded the Heisman Trophy, of course, and the Chicago Tribune Trophy as the Big Ten's most valuable player in 1954. Ironically, the only time he didn't make all-conference was after his freshman season when he set a Big Ten rushing record.

Gary Messner, all-Big Ten center and Wisconsin's captain in 1954, remembered Ameche as an opponent and a four-year teammate at Wisconsin, having played against him in high school when Messner starred at Madison East and Ameche was a standout at Kenosha Bradford.

"You had to key your defense for him or he'd run away with you," Messner said of Ameche during a 1988 interview. "He was just overpowering. He was a terrific athlete. He was a good basketball player and he threw the shot in track.

"When we were in ROTC summer camp out in Fort Eustis (Va.), he had never played ping pong," Messner remembered. "He went over, picked up the paddle and within two or three games was as good as anybody. The guy was just a natural athlete."

Ameche demonstrated his versatility as a junior and senior with a solid performance at linebacker as well as fullback after college football modified the free substitution rule.

"When they made you go two ways, he hadn't played defense since high school and he didn't have to play much then," Messner recalled. "He started working on it in the spring and by the time the season came along he was a terrific outside linebacker. He could do anything."

Ameche remembered those years fondly. "I really prided myself in my junior and senior years in trying to master that position (linebacker)," he said. "I never played it before. So, it was kind of a big challenge for me and, as I think back, those were probably my happiest years in football, including the pros, because I got to play both ways. I really felt like I was in the game. And, you were. You were in the whole game. You were in on punts, kickoffs — the whole thing."

Undoubtedly, Ameche's ability to adapt and perform so well on defense was not lost on sportswriters and sportscasters who voted in the Heisman balloting.

Thirty years after winning the Heisman, Ameche said the prestigious trophy had become more important to him as the years past. He didn't remember there being much "hype or hoopla" about it when he won the award.

"Maybe it's the fact that I'm getting old, or maybe it's the fact that the Heisman award has gotten so much more publicity, but it has taken on more meaning in recent years as I get older," he said.

The Badgers, with Ameche in the backfield, beat Iowa three of the four games they met during that era and "The Horse" earned the lasting respect of Hawkeye coach Forest Evashevski. When asked how it was facing the Wisconsin fullback, the usually curt coach exclaimed, "Oh, Ameche is a great player. He makes it so tough in setting up a defense because you've got to stop him, then you get hurt some place else."

Ameche's toughest assignments were against Ohio State. Those games, which resulted in a tie and three Badger defeats, probably frustrated "The Horse" as much as the Rose Bowl loss. Although he averaged four yards a carry against the Buckeyes in those four games, he never scored a touchdown. That was something Ohio State coach Woody Hayes always boasted about whenever he reflected on Ohio State's domination of Wisconsin during his career.

Ameche's best rushing game occurred at Minnesota as a freshman when he bolted for those 200 yards in a 30-6 victory. He drew raves, especially from Wisconsin State Journal sports editor Henry J. McCormick, who wrote after the game, "Some great fullbacks have played on this field, fullbacks like Herb Joesting, Bronko Nagurski, Sheldon Beise, Stan Kostka, Larry Buehler and Bill Daley. Fullbacks like Wisconsin's Guy Sundt, Eddie Jankowski, Howard Weiss, George Paskvan and Pat Harder. They were great ones, each and everyone, yet, it's doubtful that any of them ever put on a more impressive performance than the 18-year-old Badger from Kenosha."

Minnesota great Babe LeVoir said after watching Ameche's performance, "What a runner that Ameche is. He's got a perculiar way of running straight up, but he gets by with it." Overhearing LeVoir's remarks, Williamson, said, "I think he gets a good look at what he's doing by running straight up. It makes him a better back in the broken field."

Ameche's second best rushing production was 162 yards at Indiana in '52. That might have been his finest performance in college. He averaged 8.1 yards a carry and enjoyed his only three-touchdown game, including two on runs of 43 and 31 yards.

"The Horse" was ailing late in his senior season with leg problems. He played only 3 minutes at Illinois and never carried the ball, but the Badgers still won, 24-17. The next week at Camp Randall he appeared in his final game as a Badger. Still ailing, he carried the ball only 13 times for 26 yards.

That day, though, his teammates were determined he would go out in a blaze of glory and they dedicated probably their best overall performance of the season to him, blanking the Gophers, 27-0. When the game ended, those Badgers hoisted "The Horse" on their shoulders and carried him off the field. They and the fans in Camp Randall sensed they were seeing the end of a glorious era that might not be matched for a long time.

When Ameche left high school, some wondered if he had enough speed to make it in college football. The same doubts arose when the Baltimore Colts drafted him. Then he played a major role in the Colts' glory years.

Attorney John Walsh, former Wisconsin boxing coach who helped Ameche negotiate his first professional contract, remembers those reservations. As Walsh put it, “The pros thought they could judge his speed, but they couldn’t judge his heart.”

“He was a tremendous leader and a guy who got the job done,” Messner emphasized. “He was just sensational and a good guy.”

“The Horse” would have appreciated that epitaph.

Ameche’s career statistics follow:

College**STATISTICS**

Alan Ameche

Fullback

1951 through 1954

1951

	Att.	Yds.	Avg.	TD	Long
Marquette	1	1	1.0	0	1
Illinois	10	40	4.0	0	7
Ohio State	18	79	4.4	0	16
Purdue	25	148	5.9	1	64
Northwestern	23	124	5.4	0	34
Indiana	15	57	3.8	0	17
Pennsylvania	9	49	5.4	0	11
Iowa	25	126	5.0	1	18
Minnesota	31	200	6.5	2	42
TOTALS	157	824	5.2	4	64

1952

	Att.	Yds.	Avg.	TD	Long
Marquette	22	78	3.5	0	11
Illinois	32	116	3.6	1	13
Ohio State	25	105	4.2	0	13
Iowa	13	54	4.2	1	8
UCLA	14	31	2.2	0	8
Rice	23	116	5.0	0	23
Northwestern	31	159	5.1	0	14
Indiana	20	162	8.1	3	43
Minnesota	25	125	5.0	2	16
USC (Rose Bowl)	28	133	4.8	0	54
TOTALS	233	1079	4.6	7	54

1953

	Att.	Yds.	Avg.	TD	Long
Penn State	28	115	4.1	1	14
Marquette	21	112	5.3	2	24
UCLA	13	50	3.8	0	16
Purdue	16	58	3.6	0	9
Ohio State	16	73	4.6	0	16
Iowa	22	76	3.5	0	16
Northwestern	17	84	4.9	1	12
Illinois	17	145	8.5	0	41
Minnesota	15	88	5.9	1	13
TOTALS	165	801	4.9	5	41

1954

	Att.	Yds.	Avg.	TD	Long
Marquette	18	107	5.9	1	47
Michigan State	17	127	7.5	1	29
Rice	21	90	4.3	2	19
Purdue	18	73	4.1	1	26
Ohio State	16	42	2.6	0	9
Iowa	26	117	4.5	1	22
Northwestern	17	59	3.5	1	20
Illinois	0	0	0.0	0	0
Minnesota	13	26	2.0	2	4
TOTALS	146	641	4.4	9	47

Harland Carl

"He has little wings on his shoes and ballbearings in his joints. He is potentially one of the very finest ball-carriers in Wisconsin's history."

— *Oliver Kuechle*
Milwaukee Journal

Elroy Hirsch, Alan Ameche, Rufus Ferguson and Bill Marek attracted fans to Camp Randall Stadium, but nobody kept them on the edge of their seats like Harland Carl.

Hirsch averaged 5.4 yards per carry during his one season as a Badger, while Marek reached 5.2 during his career, Ameche 4.8 and Ferguson 3.3. Carl averaged 7.1.

A speedy, elusive halfback in the early 1950s from little Greenwood, Wis., (population about 1,100), Carl was arguably the most explosive runner ever to play for Wisconsin. Teammates called him "Hy" but writers of the day liked the ring of Harland. He scored every 10 times he carried or caught the football. Unfortunately, injuries plagued his career and he didn't touch the ball often enough.

He carried only 112 times in three years and caught just 25 passes. As a junior in 1952 on Wisconsin's first Rose Bowl team, he played only a few brief seconds near the end of the game at Pasadena because of a knee injury sustained in practice a few days before the matchup with Southern California. Many to this day feel the Badgers would have won with a healthy Harland Carl.

That was the story of his ill-fated career. The 5-foot-11, 185 pound speedster flashed his true brilliance on just a few occasions during his career.

The Harland Carl saga, which at times rivaled a Shakespearian tragedy, began when he suffered a broken navicular in his left wrist in preseason as a sophomore. The injury sidelined him for the entire 1950 season. Wisconsin fans and Badger teammates were bitterly disappointed, to say nothing of Carl himself. He had run wild against the varsity in scrimmages as a freshman and became the focus of the biggest buildup ever for a UW athlete.

"The hand injury was a freak thing," Carl explained in a 1988 interview. "It happened in a pileup (during a scrimmage). It was the navicular bone below the thumb and the dang thing still has not really healed. I have very little movement in my left hand and wrist."

Even before Carl played his first varsity game at Wisconsin, the late Oliver Kuechle, sports editor of the Milwaukee Journal at that time, wrote:

"Carl isn't a Johnny Karras or a Vic Janowicz or a Dick Athan. He isn't an Elroy Hirsch or a Tommy Harmon or a Chuck Ortman. He doesn't roar or pulverize. He doesn't pass or play defense or kick. He is just Harland Carl . . . who jitters or darts as his remarkable instinct tells him he should. He has little wings on his shoes and ballbearings in his joints. He is potentially one of the very finest ball-carriers in Wisconsin's history — certainly the most spectacular."

Remember, this deluge of superlatives came tumbling down on a small-town boy from the northland before he ever put on a game uniform. It didn't make the road any easier. But, Kuechle wasn't the only one. Dick Cullum of the Minneapolis Tribune wrote in pre-season: "Of the new men, the very best, most exciting of the season will surely be Wisconsin's Harland Carl, unless injuries take him out. . . Carl is a great runner, a touchdown-maker such as comes along only once in a great while."

Coach Ivan Williamson tried to defuse the excitement with his usual low-key approach. "He is only a sophomore," Williamson cautioned. "He needs experience — experience to loosen him up. But we think he could be great. . . They (his teammates) say he is the toughest guy to tackle they have ever faced."

These teammates weren't exactly neophytes in the art of impeding an opponent's advance toward the goal line. They developed into the fabled "Hard Rocks" that season, the school's most celebrated defensive unit.

"Being from a small school that (buildup) was kind of nice," Carl admitted. "We played a lot against the varsity as freshmen and then in spring practice and it went very well for me. That's where the buildup started. It would have been nice if they had kept it all down."

Cullum's cautious words about the possibility of injuries, though, proved prophetic. A deep thigh bruise in the 1951 opener against Marquette limited Carl's play that entire season. Then, a concussion at Iowa his junior year sidelined him for four games and recurring problems after surgery on his right knee hampered him as a senior in 1953.

Still, the swift halfback, who played six- and eight-man football early in his high school career, terrorized the opposition when healthy.

His debut against Marquette in 1951 started inauspiciously. Hounded by constant hazing from Marquette players and suffering from an acute case of rookie jitters at the outset, he managed only four yards on his first five rushing attempts. He carried only twice in the first half, gaining one yard and losing a fumble.

The record crowd of more than 46,000 (Camp Randall was enlarged from its former 45,000 capacity to 51,000 that year) started to write off Carl as another overblown phenom who could never live up to his press clippings. Then, with 5 minutes left in the game, he brought fans screaming to their feet with an electrifying 81-yard run that set up Wisconsin's second touchdown and the Badgers went on to win, 22-6.

Carl finished with 104 yards rushing that game for an average of 11.7 yards. When knocked out of bounds on that long run, though, he suffered a deep thigh bruise and it plagued him the rest of the season.

"It hemorrhaged and caused me problems the next week," Carl recalled, "but we were coming into a big game at Illinois."

He gained only 22 yards on 11 carries as the Illini handed Wisconsin a bitter 14-10 defeat that cost the Badgers a Big Ten championship. It was their only loss of the season.

"The leg was sore and I couldn't use it for two or three weeks afterward," he said. "That was a real setback. It bothered me because you think it's not a big injury but it held me back more than anything else. The knee injury I had later was in the spring and I could get it back for the season. But, that thigh bruise really laid me off and that was the year we really had a great team with the Hard Rocks."

Following the Illinois game, Carl carried the ball only four more times that season because of the leg injury. He carried three times for 30 yards and caught two passes, one for a 12-yard touchdown, in a 34-7 victory over Iowa; and he ran once for three yards as the Badgers trounced Minnesota, 30-6, the following week.

It's ironic that Carl enjoyed two of his best performances against Illinois, whose fans had ridiculed him unmercifully when he struggled with the thigh bruise in 1951 at Champaign.

The next year, when the Illini invaded Madison, their fans were ready for Carl again. They referred to him derisively as the "Jittery Jet." When he entered the game, one wag in the Illinois section shouted, "Here comes the China doll." But Carl was ready, too, and healthy this time.

"Because of all the fanfare, the Illinois fans were kind of laying for me. I had a bad game down there and they all looked forward to giving me a hard time," he shrugged.

The Badgers won that day, 20-6, with Carl rushing for 113 yards on 16 carries and scoring one touchdown. The next year Illinois again came to Madison, this time with J.C. Caroline, Mickey Bates and a 6-0-1 record. The Badgers trounced them, 34-7. It was late in the first half when Carl broke off tackle and raced 40 yards for the go-ahead touchdown. He finished with 103 yards on only seven carries for a 14.7 average, silencing his Illinois critics for all time.

"That one (1953) was the sweetest because of their great buildup," Carl reflected. "They talked about Caroline and Bates being so great but we knew Alan (Ameche) was better. It's always nice to knock off somebody like that."

As a junior in 1952 Carl opened the season with 95 yards on 10 rushing attempts against Marquette, scoring three touchdowns on runs of 11 and 52 yards and a pass that covered 53 yards as the Badgers whipped the Hilltoppers, 42-19.

Next the Badgers defeated Illinois, 20-6, and lost at Columbus to old nemesis Ohio State. Carl gained only 46 yards on 12 carries against the Buckeyes but caught six passes for 99 yards, including an 18-yard touchdown reception.

Wisconsin won big at Iowa the following week, 42-13, but the injury jinx caught up with Carl once more. He was knocked groggy late in the first half, missed the rest of the game and spent the night in the infirmary at Iowa City. Before leaving the game he gained 41 yards in six attempts, with an apparent 71-yard touchdown run nullified by a penalty, and caught a 12-yard scoring pass.

"Actually Alan's knee hit me in the back of the head as I was blocking for him on the defensive end," Carl explained. "He went right over my back and his knee hit me.

"It was a very hot day down there. I went out of the game feeling groggy but I didn't know if it was the heat or what. Then I passed out on the sidelines and the next thing I remembered I came to about 7 o'clock in the evening at the Iowa hospital. That caused me a heck of a headache for a couple of weeks."

The concussion and leg problems limited Carl's playing time the next four games and he finally got the green light for the finale against Minnesota at Camp Randall with the Big Ten championship on the line.

Although his right knee, which was operated on during the previous spring, bothered him occasionally that season, he came into the Minnesota game relatively healthy, as he demonstrated with his performance. He gained 102 yards rushing against the Gophers, including a 55-yard touchdown run in the first half, but he carried the ball only nine times, four after intermission, to the bewilderment of Badger fans.

"It kind of ticked me off, " he said. "We got into a throwing game with

Paul Giel and it ended up 21-21. We had done so well running the ball. I thought Al and I could have controlled the game running."

Writers, puzzled by Carl's infrequent use in the second half, asked Williamson after the game why his speedster was ignored. The coach replied that Harland had missed so much of the season "we kind of forgot about him." Fans didn't forget, especially after that 55-yard touchdown run in the first half. It was vintage Harland Carl. He took a pitchout, sailed around right end, cut back sharply to his left and was gone.

The game remains a classic in the long series with Carl, Ameche and Giel performing extraordinary feats. Still, it ended in a standoff and Wisconsin had to settle for a share of the championship with Purdue. An undisputed title seemed so close, and the fans filed out of Camp Randall unusually somber for such an occasion. Upon reflection, though, fans livened up later that night when realizing the Badgers did win a championship, the school's first since 1912.

Frustrations continued when the Badgers were preparing for the Rose Bowl. A few days before the game Carl twisted his right knee, which had been repaired by surgery the previous spring. The injury made banner headlines back home. The worst fears of Wisconsin fans came to pass.

"We were loosening up, doing some things on our own and I twisted it," Harland recalled. "It was one of those freakish things. It had been feeling pretty good and I'd been playing pretty well on it. Then the fluid built up and it was so fat and big at game-time I just didn't have time to get it ready again."

He saw action briefly in the waning moments of the game as the Badgers tried to overcome a 7-0 deficit. He just missed a pass in the end zone from quarterback Jim Haluska that might have tied the game.

"The defensive guy made a heck of a play," Haluska explained. "He pulled his (Carl's) arm away and the ball dropped." Badger partisans hoped they might get an interference call. It didn't happen.

Carl's senior year in 1953 went about the same as the two previous seasons. He battled the injury bugaboo throughout, carrying the ball only 32 times from scrimmage, but averaging 7.2 yards, and catching just seven passes. He did score five touchdowns and showed flashes of his old brilliance.

He seldom played defense. The limited substitution rule of that day enabled Williamson to replace certain people when the ball changed hands. However, Carl got caught on defense in the dying seconds of the Ohio State game and Buckeye great Hopalong Cassady caught a touchdown pass that nipped Wisconsin, 20-19. Carl blamed himself for the defensive lapse and was crestfallen afterward.

The following week at Homecoming against Iowa, though, he more than redeemed himself. The Badgers trailed the Hawkeyes, 6-3, with slightly more than 8 minutes to play when quarterback Jim Miller and Carl collaborated to cover 61 yards on two passes for the winning touchdown. Carl's second grab, that produced 39 yards and the touchdown, was one of the most spectacular ever seen at Camp Randall. Iowa's George "Binkey" Broeder had an apparent interception but was juggling the ball. Carl, with some Houdini sleight-of-hand, snatched the ball away and raced for the end zone.

Nobody expected Carl's heroics because he had carried only twice for seven yards and caught no passes up to that point. Williamson, the epitome of conservative rhetoric, outdid himself when asked what he thought of Carl's touchdown catch. "Mighty handy," he replied. Even he had to suppress a smile after that one.

The following week at Northwestern Carl gained 86 yards on six runs from scrimmage and had a 54-yard run for a touchdown nullified by a penalty. He also caught a scoring pass that covered 52 yards.

Poetic justice allowed him to perform spectacularly in the 34-7 trouncing of Illinois the following week, his Badger swan song at Camp Randall.

Carl later coached at Neenah High School and returned to Madison as an assistant for Milt Bruhn and John Coatta. Eventually he entered private business in Appleton.

"My Wisconsin experience was fantastic," Carl said 35 years later. "If I had to do it over, I would. If I knew then what I know now, I probably wouldn't have been as afraid to show up there. Everything seemed so large in the classes and everything else.

"I remember my first bus trip down there with one suitcase; how large it was and how afraid I was about making the team and keeping my scholarship; very much concerned about making it in the classroom; and just playing your heart out because you're from Wisconsin. I just hated to face anybody if we lost.

"I learned a lot about coaching from the Van Dykes, the Bruhns, the Williamsons. It's something I wanted to do and I did for a number of years at Neenah and then at Wisconsin.

"I just loved that whole competitive atmosphere and the winning record they started to bring into the program down there. Then playing with and meeting tremendous personnel was great. I made friends that carried through life. And, what a thrill it was to play on the same team with Alan (Ameche). He made it very simple for me."

"I think those Illinois games were my biggest thrills," Carl concluded, "but as a Wisconsin boy, just running out of that chute (at Camp Randall) was a thrill every damn Saturday. I always got worked up about that."

Dale Hackbart

"We've got a bunch of nice kids and they give us everything they've got. But, what we need is a couple of gin-drinking SOB's like Dale Hackbart."

— *Clark Van Galder*
Backfield Coach

His teammates called him "Hack" as in hacksaw or taxi. Both seem appropriate because Dale Hackbart slashed his way to football fame at Wisconsin and the Badgers rode this gridiron express to the school's first undisputed Big Ten championship in 47 years.

"Clutch player" probably was a cliche as far back as George Gipp's time but few players in University of Wisconsin football history performed at a more productive level in difficult situations than Hackbart, a quarterback in 1957, '58 and '59.

Inside an opponent's 20-yard line Hackbart was to Wisconsin what Paul Hornung was to the Green Bay Packers. Jim Mott, long-time UW sports information director, once came up with a startling statistic on the '59 Badgers, the school's first undisputed champion since 1912. He noted that every time they got inside an opponent's 20 that year they scored, mostly because of Hackbart.

He was the "big play" man television commentators tout today. When Wisconsin and Ohio State tied, 7-7 in 1958, it was Hackbart who scored the Badger touchdown on a 64-yard punt return. He ran seven yards for a touchdown when the Badgers beat the Buckeyes, 12-3, the next season and scored the touchdown in Wisconsin's 11-7 title-clinching victory over Minnesota that year.

Hackbart was part of a strong contingent of outstanding athletes who came to Wisconsin from Madison East High School. Versatility was their forte. Hackbart first gained prominence as an all-city, all-Big Eight and all-state quarterback at East. Still, basketball might have been his best game. He led the Big Eight in scoring as a senior with a 22.4-point per-game average and rebounded with the ferocity of Attila the Hun.

Or was baseball his best sport? He thought at one time of pursuing a baseball career rather than football. Besides winning three letters on the gridiron, Dale earned two in baseball and one in basketball at Wisconsin. Football dominated most of his attention but baseball seemed closer to his heart in those days.

As a senior on Dynie Mansfield's 1960 baseball team Hackbart batted .313 and led the Badgers in hits, doubles, homers, runs batted in, total bases and slugging percentage. His junior year he hit .273 and led the Badgers in triples, stolen bases and total bases.

"When I look back on it, those were the fun times in my life," Dale said in an interview 23 years after he left the university. "Actually it prepared me for a career I was unprepared for — professional football. I really looked forward to playing baseball and ended up playing football."

After graduating from Wisconsin, Hackbart spent 14 years in the National Football League as a defensive back and linebacker with Green Bay, Washington, Minnesota, St. Louis and Denver. He was a linebacker for the Vikings in Super Bowl IV.

As mentioned, though, baseball might have been his game. He tried professional baseball, too, playing a year with Grand Forks of the old Class C Northern League. One of his teammates there was Willie Stargell, who was voted into the Baseball Hall of Fame following an outstanding career with the Pittsburgh Pirates.

"I tell everybody Willie Stargell and I grew up together," Hackbart said. "A lot of memories and a lot of faces have gone in between there. I loved baseball and I just loved to play it. I signed a baseball contract with the Pirates and that's really what I wanted to do."

Wisconsin fans, though, remember Dale Hackbart mostly as the devil-may-care runner, passer, punter and defensive back who made Camp Randall an exciting stage at the height of the Eisenhower years. He played the game to win, although sometimes his aggressiveness got the best of him and he might have crossed the line of propriety on occasion.

One time when Badger football fortunes were slipping to a low ebb in the latter stages of Milt Bruhn's tenure, backfield coach Clark Van Galder was particularly depressed following a lopsided loss on the road. On the ride back from the airport he pondered Wisconsin's situation and said, "We've got a bunch of nice kids and they give us everything they've got. But, what we need is a couple of gin-drinking SOBs like Dale Hackbart."

Clark meant that as a compliment. He was just saying what a lot of people were thinking. Sometimes in athletics, especially in football, it takes a rough-and-tumble guy to intimidate the opposition and gain their respect. Pat Richter was something like that in a different way. He was a big, rangy pass-catcher who intimidated people by his presence. When the Badgers used to work out on Friday's before a road game, on-lookers from whatever town the Badgers were in would ask, "Which one is Richter?" They knew he was the guy who could give them a lot of trouble the next day.

Hackbart campaigned in the late '50s with some outstanding teammates. Guard George "Sparky" Stalcup and halfback Bob Zeman were co-captains in 1959. Stalcup was the team's most valuable player and Zeman a dependable "hitter" the Badgers looked to when things got tough on offense or defense. Tackle Danny Lanphear was a unanimous all-American in '59 and enjoyed a storybook season.

Zeman made numerous coaching stops after leaving Wisconsin and playing seven years of professional football, including a stint as Wisconsin's secondary coach under John Jardine in 1970. Coaches, especially assistants, probably often wonder about their lot in life. Zeman received the ultimate compliment from a former pupil at Northwestern, Rick Telander, a Sports Illustrated correspondent who wrote a book critical of the hypocracy in college athletics, especially football. Telander wrote in 1985 that of the 40 or so coaches he had in his life, Zeman was the finest — as a teacher and a human being.

Although a rough, tough player, Zeman was soft-spoken, even on the football field, and a sensitive person. His coaching credentials were impeccable. During his one season in charge of Wisconsin's secondary the Badgers went from 12 pass interceptions in 1969 to 22 in '70 with him coaching, to 10 in '71 after he left. This couldn't have been just a coincidence.

Zeman, Ed Hart, Billy Hobbs, Ron Steiner and Tom Wiesner were blue-collar running backs and Jim Bakken, another versatile athlete from Madison (West), backed up Hackbart at quarterback. Bob Altmann was a wingback who excelled on defense. Ends were Jim Holmes, Henry Derleth, Al Schoonover and Jim Rogers. Tackles besides Lanphear included Terry Huxhold, Jim Heineke, Lowell "Gooch" Jenkins, Brian Moore and Karl Holzwarth, who doubled as placekicker. Bob Nelson shared center with John Gotta, while Ron Perkins, Jerry Kulcinski, Don Schade and Pete Zouvas manned the guard positions with Stalcup.

Just about every one of those '59 Badgers did well after graduation, particularly Kulcinski, who belied the "dumb jock" image by becoming a distinguished professor of nuclear engineering at the University of Wisconsin. As a member of the UW athletic board he played a role in the hiring of Richter as athletic director in 1990.

Hackbart, though, became the catalyst of that championship season. It's difficult to imagine those Badgers achieving the lofty goals they set for themselves without him. A 20-9 loss at home to Iowa cost them an undefeated season and the Big Ten championship in 1958. Iowa won the '58 title with a 5-1 conference record compared with Wisconsin's 5-1-1. So, the Badgers' mission in '59 was obvious.

Hack demonstrated as a sophomore he was destined for stardom, averaging 6.1 yards a carry as the team's second leading rusher. Included in his 319 yards on 52 carries were a 57-yard touchdown run in the 41-12 victory over Northwestern and a 54-yard scoring romp as the Badgers tripped Minnesota, 14-6. He led Wisconsin against the Wildcats with 89 yards on only three carries and rolled up 99 yards against the Gophers in 11 attempts.

He also was the second-leading ground-gainer in the Marquette and West Virginia games as a sophomore, including a touchdown run of 29 yards as the Badgers trounced the visiting Mountaineers, 45-13, in Camp Randall.

The Badgers lost successive games to Iowa, Ohio State and Michigan State that season, which knocked them out of any title consideration in the Big Ten. They did share fourth place, and a 6-3 overall record wiped out much of the gloom from Bruhn's inaugural season as head coach the year before that produced an inglorious 1-5-3 log.

Hackbart turned up the heat a couple notches the next year when the Badgers fashioned their 7-1-1 mark. Again he was Wisconsin's second leading rusher with 391 yards in 101 carries and led the team in passing, completing 46 of 99 aerials for 641 yards and four touchdowns.

He also scored nine touchdowns in '58, including punt returns of 73 yards against Marquette and 64 yards in the 7-7 tie at Ohio State. He ranked among the nation's leaders, returning seven punts a total of 193 yards.

He punctuated his versatility on defense by intercepting seven passes, a school record at the time, including three in a 27-12 victory over Minnesota at Camp Randall.

Wisconsin's 1959 championship season produced a rollercoaster of emotions for Badger players, coaches and fans. It began inauspiciously with a 16-14 victory over Stanford at Camp Randall with Wiesner plunging for two touchdowns and Holzwarth booting a 26-yard field goal. Marquette football was experiencing its death throes about that time and the Badgers trounced the Hilltoppers, 44-6, the following Saturday. Hackbart passed for 160 yards and ran for two touchdowns. Hobbs also ran for a pair of scores.

Next came the first road game of the season at Purdue, where Badger morale hit the dumpster as the Boilermakers cruised to a 21-0 victory.

Len Jardine, younger brother of former UW coach John Jardine, scored two touchdowns for Purdue. Losing their first Big Ten game, and being shut out to boot, didn't enhance Wisconsin's outlook in the conference race.

"The loss to Purdue was frustrating because we were coming off a 7-1-1 season the year before and our defense was our strong point," lamented Hobbs, usually one of the most upbeat players on the squad.

The Badgers bounced back the next week to defeat Iowa, 25-16, avenging their only loss the previous season. Hobbs gained 83 yards rushing in 10 carries that afternoon against the Hawkeyes and Hackbart completed five of seven passes for 75 yards.

Ohio State arrived at Camp Randall the next week on a rainy October Saturday, the kind of weather that seemed to typify the Badger-Buckeye rivalry whether at Madison or Columbus. This was the high water mark for Wisconsin, though, because those Badgers walked off the field with a 12-3 victory and even Woody Hayes had to admit Hackbart and friends were pretty good.

The highlight of the game included the defensive play of Stalcup, Zeman and Lanphear. The latter in particular experienced an all-American afternoon. Incredibly, he put both Buckeye fullbacks, Bob Ferguson and Bob White, out of the game with savage tackles. He also started Wisconsin's scoring by blocking Ohio State's second punt attempt, the ball rolling out of the end zone for an automatic safety.

That marked Wisconsin's first victory over Ohio State since 1946 and the only time the Badgers beat a Hayes-coached team. Following the '59 victory, Wisconsin lost 21 straight to the Buckeyes before Dave McClain's 1981 team toppled them, 24-21, at Camp Randall. By that time Hayes had retired and Earle Bruce coached the Buckeyes.

Besides the safety that launched the '59 victory, the scoring included Hackbart's bootleg around Ohio State's left end for the game's only touchdown and Holzwarth's conversion as well as a 26-yard field goal. Steiner rushed for 61 yards to help control the ball that day.

Next the Badgers knocked off Michigan at Ann Arbor with Hobbs running for 70 yards and Wiesner and Hackbart scoring touchdowns. Holzwarth booted another field goal, this one for 29 yards, and Hackbart ran for a pair of two-point conversions.

This 19-10 victory over the Wolverines was particularly significant because Wisconsin had won only four times in 23 previous games against Michigan. The Badgers lost 18 and tied one. That '59 game started a streak of three straight victories over the Wolverines, a feat never accomplished by Wisconsin before or since.

The following week at Northwestern Bruhn unveiled his version of the "shotgun" or what he called the "spread" at that time. It exploited Hackbart's running and passing talents to the fullest as the Badgers outgunned the Wildcats, 24-19. This was no undermanned Northwestern team like the ones that struggled later, but an Ara Parseghian-coached outfit that featured running back Ron Burton and fullback Mike Stock, the latter an assistant coach during the Jardine era at Wisconsin. The Wildcats came into the game with a 6-0 record.

Hackbart completed five of eight passes, including a pair of scoring shots of 14 yards each to Steiner and Schoonover. He also ran for 62 yards in 10 carries. A glum Parseghian insisted the "spread" didn't surprise the Wildcats nor was it the difference in the game. He blamed Northwestern's defensive errors but conceded, "Hackbart had a great day and played a great game." Bruhn said, "Without question, this was Hackbart's finest game of the season."

The euphoria at Evanston vanished the next week at Camp Randall when the Badger morale sank to its lowest ebb since Purdue while losing the weirdest game of the season to Illinois, 9-6, before the home folks. Illini fullback Bill Brown, later a standout with the Minnesota Vikings, plunged for the winning touchdown after time had run out.

Illinois drove 81 yards in 14 plays during the last 5 minutes and 5 seconds of the game with Brown accounting for 54 of those yards on seven carries. The Illini had used up their timeouts but officials stopped the clock twice to quiet the crowd and eventually it helped the visitors score.

Wisconsin's performance was inexplicably lackluster for a team rushing headlong towards a Big Ten title. Illinois outdid the Badgers in practically every phase of the game.

Wisconsin's touchdown even came up tainted. The Badgers found themselves with fourth-and-five on the Illini 14 in the first quarter and set up for a field goal attempt. It was a fake, however. Hackbart peeled off around right end and reached the seven where he fumbled when hit. The ball squirted ahead and rolled into the end zone where Derleth recovered it for a touchdown.

The Badgers never scored again. Hackbart paced Wisconsin rushers with 65 yards and Hart added 52 but they couldn't match the Illini that day. A disenchanted crowd filed somberly out of the stadium at the end. The situation looked bleak heading for Minnesota the next week.

When Wisconsin spotted the Gophers a first quarter touchdown, fans who traveled to Minnespolis for the finale feared history might be repeating itself. Then, Altmann's pass interception set up Holzwarth's seventh field goal of the season, an intercollegiate record at that time. This gave the Badgers life and the next time they got their hands on the ball Hackbart guided them 80 yards for the winning touchdown.

A pass from Hackbart to Schoonover covering 50 yards gave Wisconsin great field position. Hack eventually scored on a keeper from one yard out and then passed to Derleth for a two-point conversion. The rangy quarterback led the way again, rushing for 74 yards and passing for 149 more besides punting once for 56 yards and intercepting a Minnesota pass.

The victory enabled Wisconsin to claim the Big Ten title by virtue of its 5-2 conference record compared with Michigan State's 4-2 and the 4-2-1 marks compiled by both Illinois and Purdue.

The Rose Bowl was anti-climactic for the Badgers after that tension-filled season. Worn down physically and mentally, they collapsed against Washington and its talented quarterback, Bob Shloredt. Although favored by 6½ points, the Badgers were humiliated, 44-8. Wisconsin's consolation touchdown came on a nine-play, 69-yard drive that featured three Hackbart passes good for 24 yards to Schoonover, 13 yards to Derleth and 20 to Zeman. Wiesner then smashed over from the four and Hackbart passed to Schoonover for a two-point conversion.

It was an ignominious experience, and writers delighted in verbally flogging the Badgers, who were accused of too much partying prior to the game. Their listless performance gave credence to those charges. Bruhn winced at the thought of that defeat for many years afterward. The next time he took a team to Pasadena, following the 1962 championship, the veteran coach kept a tight rein on their pre-game activities.

Still, the seniors on that '59 team can look back on their distinction of compiling the best three-year record in Wisconsin's modern football history — 20-6-1.

Hackbart, who led the Big Ten in total offense that year, was named all-conference quarterback and finished seventh in the Heisman Trophy balloting. He went on to play 14 years in the NFL, where he became known as a "wild and crazy" defensive back. It didn't surprise many that his career was ended by a broken neck while playing for Denver in 1973.

The '59 season doesn't conjure up visions of brilliant football that will live long in the annals of Wisconsin gridiron lore. Primarily the season spotlighted a group of smash-mouth overachievers headed by a quarterback whose blood and guts demeanor outstripped even his exceptional athletic talent. Hack was a "gamer."

Alumni Games

"Bruhn wanted to create more interest in Badger football so the Varsity-Alumni game was born."

— *Tom Butler*
Author

Once upon a time Wisconsin played alumni football games. This happened between 1957 and '61 as the windup of five spring practice sessions when Milt Bruhn was head coach.

The 1940s, '50s and early '60s probably could be considered the "golden era" of modern Wisconsin football. Elroy Hirsch, Jug Girard and Alan Ameche still were active in pro football or newly retired from the game. Bruhn wanted to create more interest in Badger football so the Varsity-Alumni game was born.

Harland Carl and Jim Haluska, big fan favorites, also came back. Ameche played only in 1957, leading the Alumni to a 35-26 victory. He carried the ball 16 times for 109 yards, a 6.8 average, and scored once on a short plunge. He was becoming a big man with the Baltimore Colts during this time and I suspect he was told not to risk his career in this type of game.

Hirsch was the marquee player in the five-year series. He caught 28 passes for 484 yards and scored seven touchdowns in the five games. That's an average of 17.3 yards a reception.

Haluska also played every game. He threw 120 passes, completed 58 for 857 yards and 10 touchdowns. He was intercepted six times. Carl appeared in the first three games. He caught eight passes for 74 yards and two touchdowns and ran 17 times for 97 yards, a 5.7 average, and scored twice. He also caught a conversion pass.

The Alumni also won the '59 game, 33-15, but the Varsity was without tackles Danny Lanphear and Jim Heineke, fullback Tom Wiesner, quarterback Dale Hackbart and halfbacks Ron Steiner, Eddie Hart and Bob Altmann. That was a pretty good nucleus of Bruhn's '59 team that won the Big Ten championship that fall.

The Varsity's three victories came in '58 by a 36-20 margin, '60 by 20-17, and '61 by 24-21. The 1958 game was played at Milwaukee County Stadium because workmen were lowering Camp Randall's field, removing the running track and increasing the stadium's capacity to 63,435.

Haluska threw two touchdown pases to Carl for 20 and 29 yards and to Hirsch for four yards in the first game. Ameche and Haluska ran for scores. Hirsch, heading into his final season with the Rams that year, caught seven passes for 83 yards. Carl grabbed five for 65 yards.

Billy Hobbs, Sidney Williams and Dale Hackbart ran for Varsity touchdowns and Williams flipped a seven-yard pass to Dave Kocourek for the other score. Jon Hobbs kicked two conversions. A crowd of 16,278 watched the inaugural game, the largest of the series.

The second game at Milwaukee attracted 11,023 and featured running touchdowns by the Varsity's Billy Hobbs, Hackbart, Bob Altmann, Jon Hobbs and Irv Partenheimer as well as a pair of two-point conversion passes from Hackbart to Williams. Hirsch scored twice on passes of 23 and eight yards from Haluska, who also tossed a conversion pass to Carl. Danny Lewis ran two yards for the other touchdown.

The game returned to Camp Randall in '59 and Alumni gridders coasted to a 33-15 victory against the depleted Varsity squad. Carl and Lewis each ran for two touchdowns before a crowd of 10,432. Dave Howard also caught a 21-yard scoring pass from Haluska. Billy Hobbs ran 22 yards for a Varsity touchdown, Dan Klinkhammer caught a six-yard scoring pass from Francis "Shorty" Young and Karl Holzwarth kicked a 13-yard field goal.

Varsity gridders bounced back with three-point victories in the last two games. The Alumni scored first in 1960 on Haluska's 51-yard touchdown pass to Hirsch. The Varsity tied the score on Ron VanderKelen's 36-yard scoring pass to Bill Kellogg in the third quarter.

Hirsch scored again in the fourth period on an eight-yard pass from Haluska, and Paul Shwaiko booted a 21-yard field goal. But the Varsity scored two touchdowns on short plunges by Neil Fleming and Tom Wiesner. The winning touchdown in the closing seconds was set up on a sensational pass reception by Ron Staley, another former Madison East athlete. Staley raced down the sidelines and caught a long pass from John Fabry for a 41-yard gain to the Alumni nine. Hirsch, playing safety, seemed to have a certain interception but Staley plucked the ball out of his hands.

Crazylegs did a "now-you-see-it-now-you-don't" doubletake and praised

Staley's athleticism after the game. Fabry passed to Merritt Norvell to the three and with time running out Wiesner blasted into the end zone on second down for the clincher.

Touchdowns on short runs by Fleming, Jim Bakken and Jerry McKinney and Bakken's three conversions and 39-yard field goal in the '61 game gave the Varsity a 24-0 lead with 7:58 remaining in the third quarter. The 80-degree temperatures seem to have wilted the Alumni but they bounced back with a vengeance.

Hackbart, throwing in '61 for the Alumni, tossed a perfect 40-yard touchdown pass to Ron Steiner with a minute left in the third quarter and Shwaiko kicked the first of his three conversions. Girard's 28-yard pass to Hirsch on a fourth-and-13 fake punt situation set up Hackbart's bomb to Steiner.

Then Hirsch showed the crowd of 9,086 what made him one of the great pass receivers in football history with two touchdowns in the final period. He took a down-and-out pitch from Haluska for 14 yards and his first tally. Then he cut to the middle and grabbed another Haluska pass that went for a 32-yard score.

Moments later the Alumni were on the way to an apparent winning touchdown when Staley intercepted another Haluska pass on the Varsity seven and returned 48 yards with less than a minute remaining in the game.

Alumni games became history after 1961 for several reasons. Mostly pro teams objected to their players participating in such contests and the Badgers themselves became leary of risking their careers with injuries. Also, Bruhn figured his squad benefitted more from an intrasquad game than an Alumni exhibition, although the latter did attract fans.

Don Kindt, a Badger star of the 1940s who retired in 1955 following a nine-year career with the Chicago Bears, did a remarkable job as coach of the Alumni during those years with assistance from such people as Hirsch, Ken Huxhold, Bob Rennebohm and Fred Negus.

Over the five years the crews of officials included such distinguished arbiters as Gene Calhoun, Richard "Bud" Lowell, Archie Morrow, Bill Cregan, Roy Bellin, Rollie Barnum, Jim Barnhill, Scott Hake, Ross Dean and even Pat Harder, who served as back judge in the '58 game.

Game summaries follow:

College**STATISTICS** 

Varsity-Alumni Game Summaries

1957 and 1958

1957

Alumni 35 - Varsity 26

	1	2	3	4	final
Varsity	7	6	6	7	- 26
Alumni	14	7	7	7	- 35

SCORING

Varsity

Billy Hobbs (run)
Dave Kocourek
(7 yd. pass from Sidney Williams)
Sidney Williams (run)
Dale Hackbart (run)
Jon Hobbs (2 PATs)

Alumni

Harland Carl
(20 & 29 yd. passes from Jim Haluska)
Elroy Hirsch
(4 yd. pass from Haluska)
Alan Ameche (1 yd. run)
Jim Haluska (run)
Glen Wilson (5 PATs)

Attendance: 16,278

1958

Varsity 36 - Alumni 20

	1	2	3	4	final
Varsity	6	14	8	8	- 36
Alumni	0	0	6	14	- 20

SCORING

Varsity

Billy Hobbs (4 yd. run)
Dale Hackbart (3 yd. run)
Bob Altmann (2 yd. run)
Jon Hobbs (5 yd. run)
Irv Partenheimer (1 yd. plunge)
Dick Meunier (PAT run)
Sidney Williams
(2 PAT passes from Dale Hackbart)

Alumni

Elroy Hirsch
(23 & 8 yd. passes from Jim Haluska)
Danny Lewis (2 yd. run)
Harland Carl
(PAT pass from Haluska)

Attendance: 11,023

College**STATISTICS**

Varsity-Alumni Game Summaries

1959 and 1960

1959

Alumni 33 - Varsity 15

	1	2	3	4	final
Varsity	0	9	0	6	- 15
Alumni	7	13	13	0	- 33

SCORING

Varsity

Billy Hobbs (22 yd. run)
Dan Klinkhammer
(6 yd. pass from Francis "Shorty" Young)
Karl Holzwarth (13 yd. field goal)

Alumni

Harland Carl (2 & 6 yd. runs)
Danny Lewis (21 & 8 yd. runs)
Dave Howard
(21 yd. pass from Jim Haluska)
Paul Shwaiko (3 PATs)

Attendance: 10,432

1960

Varsity 20 - Alumni 17

	1	2	3	4	final
Varsity	0	0	7	13	- 20
Alumni	7	0	0	10	- 17

SCORING

Varsity

Bill Kellogg
(36 yd. pass from Ron VanderKelen)
Neil Fleming (2 yd. run)
Tom Wiesner (3 yd. run)
Hank Derleth (2 PATs)

Alumni

Elroy Hirsch
(51 & 8 yd. passes from Jim Haluska)
Paul Shwaiko (2 PATs)
Paul Shwaiko (21 yd. field goal)

Attendance: 8,440

College**STATISTICS**

Varsity-Alumni Game Summary

1961

1961

Varsity 24 - Alumni 21

	1	2	3	4	final
Varsity	14	7	3	0	- 24
Alumni	0	0	7	14	- 21

SCORING

Varsity

Neil Fleming (3 yd. plunge)
Jim Bakken (8 yd. run)
Jerry McKinney (1 yd. plunge)
Jim Bakken (39 yd. field goal)
Jim Bakken (3 PATs)

Alumni

Elroy Hirsch
(14 & 32 yd. passes from Jim Haluska)
Ron Steiner
(40 yd. pass from Dale Hackbart)
Paul Shwaiko (3 PATs)

Attendance: 9,086

Pat Richter

"My dad said, 'It's got to be either sports or girls if you want to be an athlete'. . . I didn't have another date until I was a junior in high school."

— *Pat Richter*
Wide Receiver

Pat Richter traveled about two miles from Madison's East Side to attend the University of Wisconsin on a basketball scholarship and left as a record-setting pass receiver in football.

That's only part of the story. Richter experienced a storybook athletic career unmatched in UW history. The Madison native earned three letters each in football, basketball and baseball, the only UW nine-letterman since 1927. He made the all-American team at end in 1961 and '62 and was co-captain with East High teammate Steve Underwood of Wisconsin's Big Ten championship and Rose Bowl team the latter year.

Although Pat went to Wisconsin on a basketball scholarship, he was relegated to "role-player" in that sport because of reporting late each year from football. His junior year the Badgers finished second to Ohio State in Big Ten basketball, their highest standing since 1950.

Richter speculated once that baseball might have been his best sport. He hit a composite .353 at the UW and led the Badgers in hits, home runs and runs-batted-in three straight years. His tape-measure home runs were legendary at Guy Lowman Field.

Richter's biggest sports thrills came his junior year when the Badgers beat eventual Rose Bowl champion Minnesota in football, Big Ten champion Ohio State in basketball and NCAA king Michigan in baseball.

Still, football became his marquee sport. He set a school record with seven pass receptions in his first collegiate football game and gained national recognition as a junior by leading the country with 47 receptions for 817 yards. He was an imposing target at 6 feet 5 1/2 inches and 230 pounds. Ron Miller, Wisconsin quarterback in 1960 and '61, aptly described Richter's pass-catching prowess when he said, "Passing to Pat is like throwing down a funnel."

Like most great athletes, Richter had the knack of producing most significantly in key situations. He caught six passes for 142 yards and two touchdowns when the Badgers beat Minnesota in 1961. He was a standout in the 1963 Rose Bowl, catching a record 11 passes for 163 yards from Ron VanderKelen. Despite the 42-37 loss to Southern California, those Badgers gained more notoriety in defeat than the Trojans did in victory and it still is considered one of the most exciting bowl games ever played.

All-state in football and basketball, Pat attracted most state-wide attention as a rugged pivotman on East's 1958 basketball team, winner of the school's only state championship. He continued the next year as a senior, leading the Big Eight Conference in scoring.

As an East senior Pat was the lone returning letterman off the state title team but the Purgolders still went to the sectional tournament before bowing, 75-73, to eventual state champion Milwaukee Lincoln. The next night Richter scored 50 points in the consolation final against Cuba City in his prep basketball swan song.

Richter credits his dad, Pat Sr., who died in February of 1962, for influencing his athletic career "in a subtle way." He recalled, "Once in seventh grade a bunch of us took a couple girls to a movie. You know how it is at that age. When we got home my dad said, 'It's got to be either sports or girls, if you want to be an athlete.' I didn't have another date until I was a junior in high school," Pat laughed.

Glen Ralls, a physical education teacher at Marquette school, and Pat's East coaches, Butch Mueller and Verlyn Belisle, also influenced his career. "Belisle probably read me as well as anybody," Richter once reminisced. "He pushed me to get the most out of my ability. He played an important role."

Because of his glittering basketball reputation, Pat was awarded a grant-in-aid for that sport from Wisconsin. He still reported for football, though, and was elected co-captain of the Badger freshmen in 1959.

As a sophomore he caught 25 passes for 362 yards and one touchdown before breaking a collarbone in the sixth game against Michigan. This proved to be merely a temporary setback because Richter returned better than ever the following year.

The Badgers compiled a 4-2 record prior to Richter's injury in 1960 but they slumped after he was sidelined, losing to Northwestern, Illinois and Minnesota and ending the season 4-5 on the heels of the '59 championship. The record disappointed everyone but it didn't diminish the optimism for the 1961 season.

Richter rebounded exceptionally well from the broken collarbone and, after winning his first letter in basketball and hitting .398 during the Badger baseball season, he returned to the football field better than ever. His junior year turned out to be the most productive as far as statistics go. He led the nation with 47 receptions for 817 yards and eight touchdowns. He was named to numerous all-American teams and the Badgers upped their record to 6-3, including the 23-21 victory over Minnesota. Pat was a standout in that game, too, catching six passes for 142 yards and two touchdowns.

Pat once more reported for basketball following the football season and that was the year coach John Erickson put together Wisconsin's finest cage team since 1949-50, when the Badgers finished second to Ohio State in the conference.

The 1961-62 outfit also was runnerup to Ohio State, which featured Jerry Lucas and John Havlicek. The highlight of the season was Wisconsin's 86-67 victory over the Buckeyes before 13,545 fans at the Field House. It snapped Ohio State's 22-game winning streak.

Richter played no significant role in the victory but years later joked he at least made a mark in the scorebook with a personal foul. He noted that Bob Knight, the Hall of Fame coach at Indiana and then an underclassman at Ohio State, was 0-0-0 in that game.

Pat's finest college basketball performance probably came against nationally-ranked Providence in New York's Holiday Festival at Madison Square Garden. Richter scored 14 points in a reserve role as the Badgers whipped the Friars, 95-84. Wisconsin next beat Dayton, 105-93, in the semifinals but bowed to eventual NCAA champion Cincinnati in the finals, 101-71.

Pat climaxed his outstanding junior year with another fine performance with Dynie Mansfield's baseball team. That season included one of his biggest athletic thrills when the Badgers knocked Michigan out of the Big Ten championship. Pat socked two home runs in that game, one a two-run shot off Fritz Fisher with two out in the last inning. Although knocked out of the title, won by Illinois, the Wolverines came back through the tournaments and captured the NCAA championship.

"The single most rewarding moment as an individual was that Michigan baseball game," Pat said later. "I had never been able to hit that Fisher (Michigan relief pitcher) worth a damn. It was my most gratifying moment."

Richter headed into his senior year with great expectations, although it's doubtful too many people expected a championship football season, climaxed by the memorable Rose Bowl battle. Everyone wondered who would be throwing to Richter that year but Ron VanderKelen, of course, ended all speculation after the 69-13 victory over New Mexico State in the opening game.

Richter played pretty much under wraps in that first game but he did catch a pair of touchdown passes of 5 and 40 yards from Harold Brandt. He also punted once for 37 yards. The Badgers then whipped Indiana (30-6), Notre Dame (17-8) and Iowa (42-14) in succession at Camp Randall.

Pat caught five passes for 72 yards against Indiana, including one for a 3-yard touchdown from VanderKelen. He caught only two passes against the Irish, but one was for a 25-yard touchdown from Vandy.

Richter injured his right hand in the first quarter against Iowa but came back to catch six passes for 56 yards and a touchdown. He also had another apparent score in the waning moments on a perfectly-executed pass from Brandt but a penalty nullified the play.

Despite numerous spectacular plays against the Hawkeyes, coaches Milt Bruhn of the Badgers and Jerry Burns of Iowa agreed Richter's recovery of Willie Ray Smith's fumble on the kickoff following Wisconsin's first touchdown was the turning point in the game. Ron Frain deserved major credit because his jarring tackle separated Smith from the football and Pat smothered it on Iowa's 14-yard line. Ron Smith ran nine yards for a touchdown two plays later and the Badgers rolled.

The old Ohio State nemesis at Columbus bedeviled the Badgers again the following week when Wisconsin left the friendly confines of Camp Randall for the first time that season. The Buckeyes scored first in the opening period and the Badgers tied the game just before intermission on a VanderKelen to Ron Smith pass play that covered 47 yards. (Richter, hobbled by a hip injury and still nursing the sore hand from the Iowa game, managed to catch only two passes.) The Buckeyes eventually eked out a 14-7 victory with a touchdown in the fourth quarter to preserve Ohio State's mastery over Wisconsin at Columbus that extended back to 1918.

Bruhn was extremely secretive about Richter's hip injury. It was hush-hush around Camp Randall all week before heading to Columbus. Before the game UW trainer Walter "Doc" Bakke padded Pat's hip with a partially inflated football bladder for protection.

Richter was more concerned that the broken bone in his right hand would affect his ability to catch a football. He even expressed apprehension about shaking hands with Ohio State's captain during the coin toss before the game.

"If he squeezed that baby it was liable to pop all over the place," Pat fretted. "I grabbed the guy's hand as quick as I could and I grabbed his fingers. So, I was able to squeeze his fingers before he got his hand around my hand. He probably thought I was a little strange, but if he got his hand around mine, I probably would have winced and he'd know there was something wrong."

Wisconsin didn't lose again until the Rose Bowl. The Badgers swept past their next four Big Ten opponents, starting with Michigan, 34-12, at Ann Arbor a week after the disappointing loss to Ohio State. Although Richter didn't score against the Wolverines that day, he was the big man as the Badgers exploded with 20 points in the fourth quarter. Pat caught eight passes for 104 yards and several of his grabs kept Wisconsin drives going in critical situations.

Wisconsin fans caught the Rose Bowl fever the following week when the Badgers crushed a talented, unbeaten Northwestern team coached by Ara Parseghian and led by quarterback Tom Myers. The latter was completely overshadowed by VanderKelen, who now had become a household name in Wisconsin. The Wildcats breezed into town ranked No. 1 in the country and left in shock after the Badgers scored 21 points in the first seven minutes of the third quarter on the way to a 37-6 victory.

Halfbacks Lou Holland and Gary Kroner also enjoyed big games. Vandy completed 12 of 22 passes for 181 yards and three touchdowns. Holland caught two scoring passes and ran for a touchdown. Kroner tallied twice on passes and kicked a 38-yard field goal along with four conversions.

Richter didn't score. He was used mostly as a decoy when the Badgers got into scoring territory but he did lead the Badgers with five receptions for 77 yards. He also punted twice for a 42-yard average.

Naturally exuberant Badger fans resurrected the old "Rose Bowl" chant as the game progressed, much to Bruhn's chagrin. Talk of the Pasadena possibility was taboo around Wisconsin's football quarters. "When you start thinking about roses, you get into trouble," the burly coach cautioned everyone who would listen following the game.

In the gloom of Northwestern's locker room Parseghian insisted the Badgers did nothing that surprised the Wildcats. "They ran the same plays, they had the same defenses, they did everything we expected, but they did it with greater execution and with greater determination," he admitted. "In a sense they overpowered us."

Wisconsin enhanced its position in the Big Ten race with a 35-6 victory the following week at Illinois. VanderKelen and Richter didn't devastate the Illini, although Pat did punt seven times for a 40.6-yard average. This was Holland's day. The husky prep sprint champion from Union Grove scored on a 16-yard pass from Vandy and runs of 15, 18 and 35 yards. He carried the ball only four times and gained 71 yards.

That Saturday, Nov. 12, 1962, dawned cloudy and cold in Champaign. The wind whistled through Memorial Stadium, carrying with it corn leaves from fields nearby. When Bruhn sent Richter and Underwood out to take the wind if they won the coin toss, one wag in the press box complained, "You can't score if you don't have the ball."

It seemed as if he might have an argument when after six minutes the Badgers had their hands on the ball for one series with a minus nine yards to show for their efforts. Bruhn's strategy, though, provded impeccable when the Badgers took possession of the football on three more occasions before the end of the first quarter and scored each time with the wind playing a major role.

The Badgers wrapped up Wisconsin's second undisputed Big Ten title in four years the next week at home against Minnesota. It was a bizarre finish in the intense rivalry that rankles Gopher partisans to this day. A controversial roughing-the-passer penalty againt Minnesota's Bobby Bell and another 15-yard rap against Gopher coach Murray Warmath paved the way for fullback Ralph Kurek to score the winning touchdown with 97 seconds left in the game.

What Minnesota fans forget is that three straight 15-yard penalities against Wisconsin after the ensuing kickoff gave the Gophers possession on Wisconsin's 14-yard line with 72 seconds still on the clock. But, Jim Nettles' sensational interception of Duane Blaska's pass in the end zone moments later preserved Wisconsin's 14-9 victory.

Ron Leafblad and Kurek scored Wisconsin's touchdowns and Kroner kicked his 26th and 27th straight conversions. Although Richter failed to score, he again led the Badgers with six receptions for 82 yards and most of his catches helped Wisconsin control the footabll and the clock.

The 8-1 storybook season was only a prelude to the wild and crazy Rose Bowl game that occurred five and a half weeks later. The story has been told and retold many times since, how the Badgers came from a 42-14 deficit in the fourth quarter to fall agonizingly short (42-37) at the end. VanderKelen was the big story, of course, hitting 33 of 48 passes for 401 yards and two touchdowns, while also running 17 yards for a score. Richter, though, also set records with 11 receptions for 163 yards and one touchdown. The two complemented each other so magnificently they became Rose Bowl legends.

Richter remembers that people who recall that Rose Bowl game never mention that Wisconsin lost, but always talk about the great comeback. "Vandy and I went to the Hula Bowl after that and were on television with some USC players," Pat said. "They showed some outstanding plays in the game and we were kind of treated like kings. Those (USC) guys were a little bit teed off when that's all anybody wanted to talk about. They said, 'Hey, we won the game!'

"That's the way people still look at it. Several times a year somebody will remember and ask, 'Didn't you play in that Rose Bowl game?' They still remember the game."

Bruhn always credited Richter and Underwood for the leadership that enabled the Badgers to jell that year. "And, we had good people in all positions," he would quickly add.

Richter's season was capped a few days after the Rose Bowl when the Washington Touchdown Club chose him as the "lineman of the year" for which he received the Knute Rockne Memorial Award. And he was unanimous all-American.

Richter's collegiate career didn't end, though, until August when he and VanderKelen combined in the College All-Star game at Chicago's Soldier Field to upset the National Football League champion Green Bay Packers. The pair connected on a 73-yard touchdown pass that resulted in a 20-17 all-star victory.

"That All-Star game was a real thrill," Pat said. "It was my first encounter with the pros. We had scrimmaged the Bears but nobody in their wildest imagination thought we were going to knock those guys off. We knew how tough it was going to be. We saw the Packers coming off their bus for the game — McGee, Kramer and those guys. They were really kind of awesome. We were thinking, 'Oh, my God, what are we doing here?' "

But, Vandy and Richter executed the play of the game for the clinching touchdown. It was a flat pass that Pat caught at about the 50-yard line. He spun away from Packer cornerback Jess Whittenton and picked up a cordon of blockers, who escorted him the rest of the way.

"Actually, the play that beat them was called a 'Packer pass', designed for a five-yard gain," Richter explained. "It turned out to be the longest I ever had in college or pro. Going into the pros, that play was a good ice-breaker, a good respect-gainer."

Although Richter left school as Wisconsin's most prolific pass-catcher up to that time, he admitted years later he would not have been averse to playing defense during his college career.

"That was one thing I missed out on because as a freshman I loved defense," Pat explained. "I think I was probably a better defensive end than a receiver."

Pat O'Donahue, one of the famous Hard Rocks of 1951, helped coach freshmen at the time and taught Richter a lot about playing defensive end. Then Bruhn enthusiastically installed the pro-set offense about that time and Richter was a natural at split end.

"I wouldn't have been disappointed to play a standup linebacker," Pat said. "O'Donahue always kids about that. 'Hell, I got you all trained and they took you away from me,' he would say. You couldn't have had a better guy teach you how to play that position," Richter concluded.

Nobody, though, including Richter himself, would have changed anything except the outcome of the Rose Bowl. He not only was an all-American football player and nine-letterman but an exceptional advertisement for the UW. As Bruhn once said, "If there is a young man I'd pattern myself after, that would be Pat Richter. Pat has known much athletic success but his admirable personality has remained constant."

It isn't surprising the university and the public sought him so aggressively for the athletic director's job during the dark days of late 1989.

Richter's career statistics follow:

College STATISTICS

Pat Richter

Wide Receiver
1960 through 1962

1960

	No.	Yds.	TD
Stanford	7	75	0
Marquette	3	62	0
Purdue	7	110	1
Iowa	2	15	0
Ohio State	5	64	0
Michigan	1	36	0
Northwestern	Injured-Did Not Play		
Illinois	Injured-Did Not Play		
Minnesota	Injured-Did Not Play		
TOTALS	25	362	1

1961

	No.	Yds.	TD
Utah	3	23	1
Michigan State	5	60	0
Indiana	0	0	0
Oregon State	8	138	0
Iowa	3	24	0
Ohio State	6	104	1
Northwestern	7	156	1
Illinois	9	170	3
Minnesota	6	142	2
TOTALS	47	817	8

1962

	No.	Yds.	TD
New Mexico State	3	58	2
Indiana	5	72	1
Notre Dame	2	33	1
Iowa	6	56	1
Ohio State	2	41	0
Michigan	8	104	0
Northwestern	5	77	0
Illinois	1	8	0
Minnesota	6	82	0
TOTALS	38	531	5
USC (Rose Bowl)	11	163	1
All Games	49	694	6

Career Totals

No.	Yds.	TD
110	1710	14

Including Rose Bowl

No.	Yds.	TD
121	1873	15

Ron VanderKelen

"First of all he called his own plays. He was a leader, no doubt about it, and he proved his ability to lead a football team that first game."

— *Steve Underwood*
Teammate

The year 1962 was momentous. The Cuban missle crisis dominated national news, Vince Lombardi was building a football dynasty at Green Bay, and Wisconsin won its second Big Ten football championship in four seasons under Coach Milt Bruhn. Crewcuts were still in vogue, games were played on real grass and a young man of Belgian ancestry put University of Wisconsin football in national headlines.

Ron VanderKelen enjoyed probably the most fascinating rags-to-riches story in the history of college football. Notre Dame partisans insist John Huarte's rise from scrub to the Heisman Trophy winner in one year surpasses the former Wisconsin quarterback's Cinderella experience. Let's just concede it's arguable.

Think what VanderKelen accomplished from September 1962 to August of '63. Nobody before or since was named most valuable player in the Big Ten Conference, co-most valuable player in the Rose Bowl and MVP of Chicago's College All-Star game, all within a 12-month span.

Vandy won his only letter at Wisconsin during that '62 season. Before his incredible year he played only a minute and a half of college football and that as a defensive back in 1959. The All-Star game was particularly significant because VanderKelen, a Green Bay native, engineered a 20-17 victory over Lombardi's mighty National Football League champion Packers.

Life was not all roses for VanderKelen that season, though. He and Bruhn did not always see eye to eye. In fact, they had a pretty good feud going during the early part of that season.

"Milt rode me pretty hard at the beginning but there really wasn't a rift so to speak," Vandy said years later. "Somehow or other he felt that he really had to be on me. Maybe it was because he was taking a really big risk. He took a kid who had not played football at the University of Wisconsin, except for a minute and a half on defense and who had been injured and out of school for a while, and all of a sudden made him the first-team quarterback. He was putting a lot of faith in me and was obviously riding me quite hard so I didn't let down.

"Only he can answer why he was on me pretty hard. But that only lasted the first several weeks of the season. After that Milt was absolutely super to me. He could not have been nicer."

Vandy was an extremely opinionated young man and proved that later as an analyst on Badger football radio broadcasts. Hardly a shrinking violet, he had great confidence in his own ability, a trait most great quarterbacks seem to share in common.

Bruhn said he had to ride herd on VanderKelen because Ron had a tendency to "freelance" much of the time. "I had to sort of straighten Vandy out. He was a person who did his own thing quite a bit of the time. For instance, you take a fullback and dive him into the line on the first play and get some yardage. But, the next play you might get more because you fake to him and give to the halfback on the belly series.

"Well, Vandy would use the halfback first and I'd ride him. One day in practice I stopped him and said, 'Vandy, I wanted you to use that other play first and follow through with this one.' But Vandy said, 'Yeah, coach, but I got eight yards.' That's what I had to break," Milt added. "I thought I had to convince him I was running the ball club.

"I told Pat Richter and Steve Underwood (the co-captains) I was going to ride him and about the time he was ready to go back home they should let me know. One day Richter came to me and said, 'Coach, I think Vandy is ready to take off for Green Bay.'

"Then we were good to him for a while," Bruhn added with a smile. "Yeah, he was about up to Appleton," Richter chuckled. "Vandy might have been thinking, 'The hell with it. I don't need this.' Steve and I had to kind of mediate this whole thing. They (Bruhn and Vandy) weren't seeing eye-to-eye. Milt was being pretty hard on him and Vandy was about ready to chuck it or whatever."

Underwood remembered that Bruhn relied on Richter to act as his buffer between himself and VanderKelen. "I never got involved in that."

Eventually they resolved their differences and the Badgers compiled an 8-1 record, won the Big Ten championship and headed for the Rose Bowl,

The 1942 team included (left to right) in the offensive line Dave Schreiner, Paul Hirsbrunner, Ken Currier, Fred Negus, Evan Vogds, Bob Baumann and Bob Hanzlik with Jack Wink (behind center), Mark Hoskins, Pat Harder and Elroy Hirsch in the backfield.

Jug Girard weighs in at 163 pounds after the 1944 season.

Jug Girard returns a punt for a touchdown against Iowa in 1947.

Mark Hoskins, one of the "Three-H Boys" in the 1942 backfield.

Pat Harder (34) ready to spring Elroy Hirsch (40) on a 59-yard run against Ohio State in 1942.

The "Hard Rocks" were
Wisconsin's most celebrated defensive unit.

Alan Ameche heads upfield behind Clarence Stensby and George Steinmetz.

Alan Ameche blasts for a gain against Iowa in 1953.

Victorious Badgers carry Alan Ameche off the field on their shoulders after his final game in 1954.

Red Wilson catches a pass against Navy in 1949.

Speedy Harland Carl darts away from a would-be tackler.

Pat Richter grabs a pass for a 56-yard gain against Illinois in 1961.

Ralph Kurek plunges for a touch-down in the 1963 Rose Bowl.

Pat Richter set a record with 11 receptions in the 1963 Rose Bowl.

Carl Silvestri caught 3 passes for 51 yards in the 1963 Rose Bowl.

Ron VanderKelen (right) and Merritt Norvell show their disappointment in the waning seconds of the 1963 Rose Bowl game.

Jerry Stalcup (60) prepares to block for Dale Hackbart.

Fans carry coach John Coatta off the field after the 1969 Iowa game.

Dennis Lick is considered by many Wisconsin's best offensive tackle ever.

Center Mike Webster was Wisconsin's MVP in 1973.

Rufus Ferguson skips away from four Buckeyes in Camp Randall.

Billy Marek breaks away on a 54-yard touchdown run against Northwestern in 1975.

Randy Wright passes under pressure against Illinois in 1983.

Al Toon makes a sensational catch during his record-setting performance at Purdue in 1983.

Jess Cole caps a 52-yard touchdown run against Minnesota in 1980.

Dave Mohapp protects quarterback Mike Kalasmiki.

Tim Krumrie takes aim at a Purdue ballcarrier.

Matt Vanden Boom and David Greenwood celebrate after Matt's pass interception against Michigan in 1981.

where Vandy turned in one of the most fantastic bowl performances seen anywhere.

The '62 championship shouldn't have been too surprising. The Badgers compiled a 6-3 record the year before, but 1961's quarterback, Ron Miller, was gone. Bruhn had to depend on an untested signal-caller no matter whom he chose. That's what made the run for the roses such a shock. First year-quarterbacks seldom develop that quickly.

Most figured Bruhn's quarterback would come from a threesome that included sophomore Harold Brandt, senior John Fabry and junior Arnie Quaerna. In fact, the author and Wisconsin State Journal photographer Ed Stein on picture day set up a shot that featured seven prospective quarterbacks squiggled in the shape of a question mark with center Ken Bowman as the dot. The seventh and last player at the end of the loop was Vandy. So much for our insight.

Richter, a consensus all-American end that year who later left the world of law and business to become UW athletic director, didn't consider the '62 season a total surprise. He once reflected that the foundation for '62's success was laid during a 23-21 victory over Minnesota at Minneapolis in the last game of the 1961 season.

"That was really an exciting game and an exciting time," Pat said. "There were a lot of guys like Jim Bakken and Dick Grimm who were seniors. It was such a kick for them to beat a team that had won the championship and was going to the Rose Bowl. I think it brought a lot of guys together. We thought, 'Hey, this is a pretty good ballclub.' And, we didn't lose a lot of guys off that team and the freshmen coming up were bigger than we had before. I don't think it necessarily was a surprise, nor did we expect it. It just sort of happened."

The emergence of VanderKelen did surprise everyone, however. Nobody envisioned Vandy as the heir apparent, and who possibly could have predicted the level of excellence VanderKelen achieved during his senior year. Certainly not Richter.

When Ron Miller, who quarterbacked the Badgers the previous two years, didn't receive another season of eligibility as Bruhn had hoped, team members expected Fabry to inherit the job. VanderKelen was almost a nonentity as far as Richter was concerned. Vandy sat on the bench as a sophomore reserve quarterback during the championship season of 1959 and at the Rose Bowl. He missed the 1960 season because of knee surgery and dropped out of school in the fall of '61. He re-enrolled the following January and was given another year of eligibility because of the knee injury. After practicing that spring, he was ready for the fall.

"I don't remember him being there until he came on that senior year," Richter said. "I don't remember him even practicing," added Underwood. "I'm sure he did but to my mind he was never there. He was a total stranger to the team."

Bruhn wasn't that surprised. "Not really," he said. "We thought we had a pretty good thing going, especially when VanderKelen developed as well as he did during the summer months."

Bruhn credited a drill he learned from Vince Lombardi for much of VanderKelen's improved passing. The quarterback stood between the hashmarks and had two receivers go straight downfield. He took two steps, brought the ball up in the same motion and threw to one of the receivers.

Vandy wound up leading the Big Ten in passing and total offense and received the Chicago Tribune Trophy as the conference's most valuable player. He passed for 1,181 yards and 12 touchdowns, while also running for 252 yards (second only to fullback Ralph Kurek on the team) and a pair of touchdowns.

The Badgers opened that season by trouncing New Mexico State, 69-13. The Aggies were a late entry on Wisconsin's schedule, replacing Marquette, which dropped football after the 1960 season. They added victories over Indiana (30-6), Notre Dame (17-8) and Iowa (42-14) before traveling to Ohio State, where the Badgers bowed, 14-7.

They bounced back with a victory at Michigan (34-12), showed they were for real by shellacking the nation's No. 1 team at the time, Northwestern (37-6), and sealed their title by whipping Illinois (35-6) and downing Minnesota (14-9).

VanderKelen made his debut in the opener against New Mexico State, completing five of eight passes for 150 yards, including a scoring pass to Lou Holland that covered nine yards. Bruhn used 62 players that day, including three other quarterbacks — Brandt, Fabry and Greg Howey.

"We went into the first game not really knowing at all what kind of a football team we had," Underwood recalled. "VanderKelen set the stage right there. First of all he called his own plays. He was a leader, no doubt about it, and he proved his ability to lead a football team that first game. Everybody gained confidence in him. We were off to the races."

Richter contrasted the difference between Miller, the quarterback his first two years, and VanderKelen. "Ron (Miller) was easier to get along with than Vandy. They were different personalities. Miller was more easy going."

He added that as Vandy developed and the team improved confidence grew. "You can acquire confidence in a quarterback but if you didn't have the other supporting characters, you really woudn't be able to pull it off. We had those young guys who were so big — (Al) Piraino, (Roger) Jacobazzi and (Roger) Pillath — mixed with (Jim) Schenk and (Steve) Underwood. You had a massive bunch of guys who were pretty good athletes, too. All it needed was a spark." VanderKelen provided that.

Bowman, later a standout center for the Green Bay Packers, explained VanderKelen's leadership this way: "If we needed five or 15 yards on third down, he convinced us in the huddle we'd get it and we would."

Vandy completed seven of 10 passes against Indiana for a modest 96 yards, with a three-yard toss going to Richter for a touchdown. He sparked the 17-8 victory over Notre Dame with a 25-yard scoring pass to Richter and a one-yard sneak for another touchdown. He completed eight of 14 passes for 122 yards and also intercepted an Irish pass while playing safety.

The following week he threw touchdown passes to Elmars Ezerins, Ron Smith and Richter in the romp over Iowa. The Badgers jelled in this game and Vandy explained: "It was one of those situations that occasionally happens in sports where the chemistry was right among all team members.

"There was a fair amount of talent on the team, but what happens a lot of times is you can have individual talent on a team, even great talent, but you can't win because the chemistry isn't right. We were a team that was able to get along very well together. Somehow or other the more we played together the more cohesive as a group we became. Nobody predicted Wisconsin would do well that year. I don't even think the coaching staff felt we were going to do that well."

The trip to Ohio was like so many taken by Badger teams since 1918, which was the last time Wisconsin had won there. The '62 Badgers went down to defeat, 14-7, the only touchdown coming on VanderKelen's 47-yard pass to Ron Smith just before halftime. Vandy completed only seven of 22 throws against a secondary led by Buckeye ace Paul Warfield.

Undaunted, the Badgers rebounded at Michigan with a 34-12 victory that convinced most doubters this team was a serious contender. All five Badger touchdowns came on short plunges, but Vandy spearheaded the drives by completing 17 of 25 passes for 202 yards and running 13 times for 59 yards and one touchdown. Richter caught eight passes for 104 yards.

The Badgers demolished top-ranked Northwestern the following week. Vandy caught the fancy of football fans nationally against the Wildcats. He was a great scrambler and threw accurately on the run, completing 12 of 22 passes for 181 yards and three touchdowns, two to Gary Kroner and the other to Holland, who also ran for two scores.

A dark and windy day at Illinois on the second to last game of the season didn't bother the Badgers as they romped past the Illini, 35-6. This day belonged to Holland.

The wind-swept gridiron made passing hazardous and Vandy completed only six of 16 for 81 yards and one touchdown. He did run five times for 48 yards.

The title-clinching game against Minnesota on the hallowed Camp

Randall grounds produced just about the wildest action in the long Badger Gopher series. It was debated and rehashed for two decades afterward and continues to rankle long-of-tooth Minnesota fans to this day. No matter how the game is dissected, though, it always comes out a 14-9 Wisconsin victory.

Nov. 24, 1962, dawned near perfect for football with temperatures in the 40s and a 5 mph wind out of the south. Minnesota players, who left snow-covered Minneapolis, romped like frisky colts when they got the feel of Camp Randall's lightning-fast gridiron. They had all the best of it statistically in the game, picking up 21 first downs to 14 for Wisconsin and rolling up 353 total yards to 219 for the Badgers.

Minnesota scored first in the second quarter on a 15-yard pass from quarterback Duane Blaska to halfback Jim Cairns. Collin Versich's conversion attempt sailed wide. The Badgers took the ensuing kickoff and drove 65 yards with VanderKelen passing 13 yards to end Ron Leafblad for the touchdown with 10:15 remaining in the first half. Gary Kroner's conversion gave the Badgers a 7-6 halftime lead.

Versich atoned for his missed conversion by booting a 32-yard field goal with 4:49 left in the third quarter. Then the Badgers fumbled away their next two possessions. In fact, Holland fumbled a Gopher punt and Minnesota recovered at Wisconsin's 36 on the last play of the period. Fortunately for the Badgers, Billy Smith intercepted Blaska's pass three plays later to avert a catastrophe.

Wisconsin managed just one first down on its next two possessions and it appeared as if the Badgers had run out of steam after their arduous campaign. Still, VanderKelen marshalled his forces in one more heroic charge for which he was becoming famous.

Minnesota punted into Wisconsin's end zone with 3:54 left in the game and the Badgers launched their winning drive from their own 20. After Vandy's first pass fell incomplete, he hit Richter for 12 yards. The drive lost a little momentum when Carl Eller sacked Vandy for a five-yard loss on the next play.

Another pass fell incomplete but Vandy then connected with Richter for 18 and 12 yards for a first down on Minnesota's 43. What followed must be considered one of the wildest and most controversial plays in this long series.

Jack Perkovich intercepted VanderKelen's next pass but Gopher tackle Bobby Bell was flagged for "roughing" the Wisconsin quarterback. The Gophers, who had been working Vandy over vigorously throughout the game, lost 130 yards on 14 penalties. Wisconsin was tagged eight times for 88 yards.

A storm of protest erupted on the Gopher side of the field following this one. Tempers flared. Minnesota coach Murray Warmath protested so vehemently that referee Robert Jones tacked another 15 yards onto Bell's penalty. When calm, such as it was, settled over the field, the Badgers found themselves with a first down on Minnesota's 13 and 2:25 on the clock.

VanderKelen recalled the Bell incident: "That was a very physical day. I had been bounced around all day long. I ran the ball quite a bit. I was chased out of the pocket quite a bit. So, as we got near the end of the game I was pretty beat up. One more punch really didn't make any difference.

"I honestly can't tell you whether he hit me or not illegally. The only thing I remember about the play was that as I dropped back to pass and threw the ball, I saw the flag go down. I knew there was a penalty and, of course, I saw the interception. But I saw the referee signaling that Bell had thrown an elbow across my face which was the reason, I think, he called the penalty."

Bell said after the game that head linesman Don Elser told him, "You roughed him all the way down." Bell responded: "How could I rough him? I made a high tackle going for the ball and I hit it. I got up in time to see the guy intercept the ball."

Following the penalties, Holland circled right end to the eight and VanderKelen gained six more for a first down at the two. Kurek fought his way into the end zone on the next play with 1:37 left. The frenzied crowd of 65,154 (capacity at the time) then watched Kroner kick his 27th straight conversion.

Plenty of time remained for the Gophers and subsequently they were aided and abetted by the officials, who were struck with a sudden attack of the ancient "let's-even-it-up" syndrome following Warmath's tirade. The Badgers were charged with an unsportsmanlike conduct penalty on the kickoff and two pass interference raps on the next three Gopher passes. Quickly Minnesota had first down on Wisconsin's 14. The "fat lady" started vocalizing, though, when Jim Nettles intercepted Blaska's next pass in the end zone with 59 seconds left.

Nobody left the stadium, though. The Badgers managed only two yards on their next three plays and were socked with another unsportsmanlike penalty back to their 11. Richter then boomed a 51-yard punt to Minnesota's 39 with 17 ticks still remaining. The Gophers completed one more pass to the 50 before the clock ran out. It was party time.

Not everybody was celebrating, however. A small group of irate Minnesota fans, upset by the officiating, caught up with the five stripedshirts as they raced off the field. One fan jumped on the back of an official but police quickly restored order and escorted the harried arbiters to their locker room in the Field House.

Old grudges die hard and this one festered for years. Some Minnesota fans later sent a poignant cartoon to Wisconsin State Journal columnist Roundy Coughlin. It depicted a group of Wisconsin football players carrying an official off the field on their shoulders. The caption read: "Judgment at Madison." Roundy framed the artwork, which hung on the wall of his little office on Carroll Street until the day he retired.

What Gopher fans conveniently forget is that Minnesota was the recipient of 60 yards in penalities following Kurek's touchdown. The Gophers didn't capitalize on their good fortune. It boiled down to Minnesota's inability to contain VanderKelen and Richter who combined for 82 yards on six passes, most of them in critical situations.

Vandy's epic wasn't finished, though. The Rose Bowl and Chicago's All-Star game were yet to come.

THE Rose Bowl

"You cannot dream the kind of game I had in the Rose Bowl. . . We just jelled as a team and were very explosive offensively."

— *Ron VanderKelen*
Quarterback

The genesis for Ron VanderKelen's sensational 1963 Rose Bowl performance can be traced to Wisconsin's 44-8 loss at Pasadena three years earlier, when he rode the bench as a reserve quarterback and safety. Vandy sat there and watched Wisconsin's Big Ten champions disintegrate before an onslaught by Washington's Huskies. He never forgot that nightmare nor wanted to experience such an humiliation again.

"It was like a massacre," Ron remembered. "We let down real bad. That was a senior team and only about 18 guys played a lot. By the end of the season they were worn down. Then Washington hit us fast and we just couldn't catch up with them."

Three years later he found himself on the turf in that historic Arroyo Seco stadium, this time as a key participant against the No. 1-ranked Trojans of Southern California. A victory would have vaulted Wisconsin to a national championship because the Badgers were ranked No. 2 in the Associated Press poll.

A crowd of 98,698 turned out for the 49th Rose Bowl game on a cloudy dark afternoon. The kickoff was delayed 15 minutes because of numerous special ceremonies and introductions. Wisconsin players languished on the sidelines during this time, while the Trojans remained in their locker room until almost the last minute. Some Badgers attribute their slow start to warming up and then cooling down during the delay.

USC drove for a touchdown on its first possession before the Badgers got untracked. Following two fruitless possessions, Wisconsin finally drove 81 yards in 11 plays to tie the score at 7-7 on fullback Ralph Kurek's one-yard plunge and Gary Kroner's conversion. VanderKelen completed five passes for 38 yards along the way.

The Trojans scored on their first two possessions of the second quarter for a 21-7 lead, while the Badger offense sputtered. With time running out in the first half, VanderKelen connected on two passes to Larry Howard and Lou Holland for 33 yards to Southern Cal's 30. Then Vandy found Holland again for an apparent touchdown but an official called a clipping penalty on the Badgers, nullifying the score. Vandy's next pass fell incomplete as time ran out.

"I still feel there wasn't a clip on Louie Holland's run," coach Milt Bruhn insisted years later. "I think he (the official) was goaded into calling that by Johnny (McKay, USC coach)."

VanderKelen seemed to catch fire late in the first half but the long intermission stole his momentum and the Badgers started the third quarter with some apparent lethargy.

The Trojans struck quickly on the first play of the second half. Pete Beathard hit end Hal Bedsole on a slant pattern and the fleet Trojan end raced 57 yards for a touchdown.

"I felt between halves that we had found something in Southern Cal's defense," Bruhn remarked. "Then Bedsole caught a pass and went across the field and down for that touchdown. That knocked us for a loop for about 10 minutes and we had to get our bearings again. If he hadn't done that, I'm sure we would have won. It took 10 minutes from us. And, we had 'em going toward the end of the game."

Actually, Vandy didn't waste that much time. He led the Badgers 67 yards in eight plays, cutting Wisconsin's deficit to 28-14. He completed three passes for 36 yards and did a masterful job of scrambling 17 yards for the touchdown.

But, Southern Cal scored again before the end of the third quarter and once more 6 seconds into the final period for a 42-14 lead. This looked like 1960 and Washington all over again. VanderKelen, who still felt the sting of that rout, determined it wouldn't be repeated.

The dim stadium lights, which were turned on at halftime, were casting an eerie glow over the field by this time. The teams played in semi-darkness during the closing minutes.

The ensuing kickoff sailed into the end zone and the Badgers started from their own 20. Kurek gained four on first down and then VanderKelen threw nine straight passes, completing seven for a first down at the Trojan 13 from where Holland scored on a pitchout.

Then on first down following the kickoff, Lee Bernet crunched USC fullback Ben Wilson, forcing a fumble that Elmars Ezerins of the Badgers recovered on USC's 29. Vandy found Richter for 19 yards on first down, Holland circled right end to the six, Jim Purnell rammed to the four and Vandy passed to Kroner for the touchdown. Following Kroner's conversion, the Badgers trailed by only 14 again, 42-28.

Wisconsin fans relaxed somewhat, convinced the Badgers at least were making a game of it. That wasn't enough for VanderKelen. The Badgers weren't conceding anything. The Trojans made one first down on their next possession and were forced to punt. Wisconsin took over on its 32 and five straight completions by Vandy gave the Badgers a first down on USC's four-yard line. Here disaster struck. VanderKelen threw a pass into the end zone on first down and USC's Willie Brown intercepted.

Bruhn would like to have sent Kurek into the line or Holland around end on first down, but Vandy thought he was holding too hot a hand. The coach once called that play the only mistake in the game by VanderKelen.

Vandy said his receiver, who was not a regular, had to share the blame because he stopped and didn't complete his route to the corner of the end zone as prescribed. "There was nobody there but a Southern California player, and he picked it off," Ron shrugged. "If we had scored there, we would have won the game. Later, when I threw to Pat on a slant-in, he took it all the way (19 yards with 1:19 left). That one would have won the ball game."

The Trojans gained only five yards on three plays and when the center snap sailed over punter Ernie Jones' head on fourth down, Badger tackle Ernie von Heimburg tackled him in the end zone for a safety. The score now was 42-30 with 2:40 remaining.

Ron Smith returned the free kick 21 yards to the Trojan 43, and Vandy quickly rallied his forces. He passed to Holland for six yards, to Richter for 18 and to Pat again for 19 and the touchdown with 1:19 left. Kroner's conversion pulled the Badgers within five points at 42-37.

The Trojans recovered Kroner's on-side kickoff at their 41 but lost 12 yards in three plays. Ezerins just missed blocking Jones' punt. Holland fumbled the return but UW guard Jim Schenk recovered on Wisconsin's 48. Time ran out before the Badgers could snap the ball again. VanderKelen always felt he needed only about 25 more seconds to get into the end zone again.

The tension and frenzy of the fourth quarter left players and fans on both sides limp at the end. Everybody knew they had witnessed one of the great bowl games in history. Southern Cal exhaulted. Wisconsin was left to ponder what-might-have-been. The Badgers even came within an eyelash of blocking the final punt. The ball sailed under the armpit of Ezerins.

"We should have blocked that punt," Underwood lamented. "Then

Cinderella couldn't compare to our story."

And there were other "what ifs" to ponder. The delays. The "phantom" penalty that nullified Holland's touchdown just before intermission. Maybe VanderKelen should have run the ball himself from the four instead of passing. And, why did the officials take 25 seconds off the clock late in the game? The Badgers seemed to have done so much. They didn't deserve a loss.

This was a talented team. Not only were these Badgers explosive offensively, averaging more than 32 points a game, they hit on defense and limited opponents to less than 10 points a game during the regular season.

During this era only two substitutions could be made after each play. Bruhn used two strong defensive ends, Ron Carlson and Larry Howard, for Richter and Ron Leafblad. VanderKelen usually stayed in at safety for one play. Ken Bowman played center. Underwood, Schenk, von Heimburg, Dion Kempthorne and Jon Hohman shared the guard spots. Roger Pillath, Lee Bernet, Andy Wojdula and Roger Jacobazzi saw most action at tackle. Jim Nettles and Ron Frain patrolled the secondary exclusively. Fullbacks were Kurek, Merritt Norvell and Jim Purnell, the latter two rugged linebackers also. Halfbacks besides Holland and Ron Smith were Carl Silverstri, Rick Reichardt, Billy Smith and Kroner, also the placekicker.

"There wasn't a weak position," Underwood said. "Even right guard (his spot) wasn't weak."

VanderKelen put up Rose Bowl record numbers that day, completing 33 of 48 passes for 401 yards and two touchdowns. The attempts, completions and yards are still school records, as well as his 406 yards total offense in that game. He completed 69 percent of his passes and in the second half alone connected on 22 of 29 throws for 269 yards (.759 accuracy). Richter caught 11 passes for 163 yards, also Rose Bowl records at the time.

USC quarterback Pete Beathard was voted most valuable player of the game during balloting early in the fourth quarter, which usually is routine procedure for TV purposes. When Vandy's statistics began to mount and USC's margin shrunk, another vote was taken. It was determined the two quarterbacks should split the honor.

"You cannot dream the kind of game I had in the Rose Bowl," VanderKelen reflected. "It was one of those series of events like the Wisconsin team was having all year. We just jelled as a team and were very explosive offensively. We had a lot of super offensive weapons."

Underwood remembered that wild fourth quarter vividly. "At one point I was kind of in a fog. I remember being so down mentally after three quarters and then just being part of something happening that was almost magical and wondering whether it was a dream."

Many detractors to this day say, "Yes, but it was a loss. There's no such thing as a moral victory." But, that's not entirely true. Idealists insist there is more to athletics than winning. These Badgers struggled for three quarters but wouldn't concede. They scored 23 points in the last 11 minutes. One "mistake" and a questionable clipping penalty cost them the ball game. It was cruel, yes, but VanderKelen and the '62 team created a UW football mystique that endured for years afterward.

However, the saga didn't end at Pasadena. Vandy and Richter traveled to Honolulu the next week and the Badger quarterback passed 17 yards to Washington State end Hugh Campbell for the winning touchdown as his North squad defeated the South, 20-13, in the Hula Bowl.

Next came the Coaches' All-American game at Buffalo in June before VanderKelen and Richter headed for the "big one" at Chicago in August. Their performance against the Packers could hardly be called anticlimactic. The game became another incredible chapter in the VanderKelen saga.

He and Richter humbled the mighty Packers by combining on a 73-yard touchdown pass in the fourth quarter for a 20-17 All-Star victory. Richter caught the ball on the 50, spun away from cornerback Jesse Whittenton and headed for the end zone with a cordon of blockers assuring safe passage.

VanderKelen set up an earlier touchdown with a 21-yard toss to Richter and clinched the game's most valuable player award with those two clutch plays and 141 yards on nine completions in 11 attempts. Vandy later enjoyed fair success in the NFL with the Minnesota Vikings while playing behind Fran Tarkenton, but matching his collegiate experience was next to impossible. He became a Wisconsin legend in 10 games and then carried the Badger banner in one more glorious moment as a College All-Star.

The Drought

"Inevitably there is a direct correlation between recruiting and won-loss records and recruiting was difficult during this era."

— *Tom Butler*
Author

Following the 1963 Rose Bowl, Wisconsin football fortunes started sliding into obscurity. The Badgers reached the crest of the heady Williamson-Bruhn years with the 1962 Big Ten chiampionship. The decline began during the 5-4 season of '63 and lasted for a decade.

Bruhn's Badgers won their first four games in '63 and then dropped a 13-10 decision to Ohio State at Camp Randall in a game they were supposed to win. The Buckeyes were ailing. Wilbur Snypp, Ohio State sports information director, told Madison Pen and Mike Club members the previous Tuesday that big fullback Matt Snell couldn't navigate the campus without crutches. Snell represented a major portion of Woody Hayes' celebrated Ohio State power attack.

Well, between the time of Snypp's gloomy prognosis and the kickoff on Saturday, Snell experienced a miraculous recovery. He toted the ball 24 times against the Badgers, gained 93 yards and carried the Buckeyes to victory despite the exploits of Wisconsin's Lou Holland and Carl Silverstri, who ran for 95 and 79 yards, respectively.

Wisconsin traveled to Michigan State the next week and lost to the Spartans, 30-13. The UW decline can be traced directly to that defeat at East Lansing Nov. 2, 1963. The Badgers beat only Northwestern, 17-14, in their last five games that season. Excitement generated in that 1949 victory over Marquette, the start of the Williamson era, finally subsided.

Fun, games and large crowds became memories.

Bruhn, the only Wisconsin coach ever to win two Big Ten championships, was forced to resign in 1966 following three straight losing seasons. His "resignation" came before the Minnesota game and his Badgers gave him a 7-6 victory in his swan song.

Some blamed Bruhn's decline to losing recruiting advantages he enjoyed in the Chicago area. Part also can be traced to the Big Ten's ill-advised decision in 1956 to award scholarships on the basis of need. The conference later rescinded that decree but Big Ten football teams suffered irreparable damage to their recruiting for years afterward. Such neighboring conferences as the the Big Eight gleefully profited from the Big Ten's unilateral sanctimony.

Bruhn was a popular coach and the announcement upset his players. Senior defensive end Eric Rice said, "I don't know of anybody I have more respect for than Coach Bruhn except my own father."

The 3-6-1 record that year overshadowed some fine individual performances. Linebacker Bob Richter, the team's most valuable player, made all-Big Ten and wide receiver Tom McCauley caught 46 passes.

John Coatta, a record-setting Badger quarterback in 1951 and one of Bruhn's assistants, succeeded him as head coach. The old bromide about being caught in the wrong place at the wrong time aptly describes Coatta's three-year tenure. It turned into a disaster. Hopes for success glimmered in 1969 but the harried head coach was dismissed after the season by new athletic director Elroy Hirsch, who assumed his duties the previous February.

The Badgers lost nine games and tied Iowa, 21-21, in 1967. It was the kind of a season where the record might have wound up 5-5. The Badgers lost to Pittsburgh, 13-11; to Northwestern, 17-14; and at Ohio State, 17-15. The term "snake bit" might have originated during this season.

An example of the kind of season it was occurred during the Indiana game at Bloomington. The Hoosiers eventually shared the Big Ten championship and played in the Rose Bowl. They defeated Wisconsin along the way, 14-9. The Badgers led in first downs, 20-17, and outgained Indiana in total yards, 335-268. Wayne Todd, a pile-driving fullback, enjoyed a banner day, repeatedly riddling Indiana's defense.

Wisconsin, trailing, 14-3, was driving in the fourth quarter with Todd carrying the ball seven out of 11 plays. His last surge off left tackle gained 17 yards to the Indiana seven. But "Hot Toddy," as Coatta called him, broke his thumb on the play, left the game, and the drive fizzled.

Gale Bucciarelli replaced Todd and sparked another drive, which quarterback John Boyajian culminated with a two-yard touchdown run. A two-point conversion pass failed but the Badgers regained possession with 2:08 left and drove once more, winding up on the Hoosier 10 with 4 seconds left. Boyajian's final hurried pass into the end zone sailed over Mel Reddick's head. The Badger quarterback might have been somewhat confused, though, because inexplicably a photographer was standing next to Reddick in the end zone at the time.

That "can't-win-for-losing" syndrome hung precariously over Wisconsin's head, and 1968 became even more disastrous. The Badgers lost 10 straight games, including three shutouts in a row. Attendance slumped and fewer than 45,000 were attending home games. Wisconsin coaches seldom survive when crowds decline.

Inevitably there is a direct correlation between recruiting and won-loss records, and recruiting was difficult during this era. Anti-war protests and a black boycott of the 1968 football banquet led many parents to consider the UW campus an unhealthy environment for their offspring. The late George Martin, then Wisconsin's wrestling coach, recruited almost exclusively in-state and often expounded on his difficulties during these unsettled times.

Coatta and his football program suffered along with other sports on campus. During one stretch the National Guard, patrolling the campus, was headquartered at the Stadium. Just about everybody, including Coatta, needed a pass to get near the area. Years later John could laugh about such an incongruous situation but it wasn't funny at the time.

Despite the 0-19-1 record Wisconsin coaches and players started preseason practice in 1969 with unusual optimism. Coatta was convinced he possessed some offensive tools to break the long winless streak.

These offensive weapons surfaced in the opening game against Oklahoma in Camp Randall but the Sooners still tacked on another loss (42-21) to the Badger record. Alan "A-Train" Thompson, a quick, powerful fullback, outdid Oklahoma's eventual Heisman Trophy winner Steve Owens, 220 yards to 189, and established a UW single game rushing record in that game.

The Badgers made another strong showing at home against UCLA the following week but again the result was the same, a 34-27 defeat. Wisconsin players were upbeat in the locker room afterward and somebody started singing "On, Wisconsin!" A chagrinned Coatta would have none of that and insisted, "We weren't singing and we won't until we do win."

Wisconsin prepared for the next game against Syracuse enthusiastically. Incredibly, Badger fans around town and even the players themselves seemed wrapped in an aura of self-confidence. More specifically it was over-confidence. Larry Kimball, Syracuse sports information director, commented on this strange phenomenon years afterward. He couldn't imagine what he encountered upon arriving in Madison four days before the game. "How could a team, winless in 22 straight games, be over-confident? " he mused.

Well, the Orangemen shattered Wisconsin's grandiose illusions by trouncing the Badgers, 43-7. When Syracuse capped the day with a two-point conversion following its last touchdown, Wisconsin players felt their noses were being rubbed rudely into the Camp Randall turf. Two plays following the next kickoff, a fight broke out. Players left their respective benches and the ensuing free-for-all ranks as probably the ugliest confrontation of its kind ever seen at Camp Randall. Two minutes after order was restored the game ended and the Badgers trudged back to their locker room with heads bowed and confidence wavering once more.

The bravado so evident the previous week disappeared, but not the resolve, during the practice for Iowa, the fourth straight home game. Syracuse knocked the Badgers back to reality. The Hawkeyes were coming into the game with victories over Washington State and Arizona and a loss to Oregon State. Coatta and the Badgers realized another struggle awaited them.

Iowa took command early and the Badgers entered the fourth quarter trailing, 17-0. Fans seemed resigned to another disappointment. But the Badgers were driving at Iowa's 20 heading into the final period. They scored what seemed to be a consolation touchdown with 12:26 left in the game. Thompson plunged two yards for the score, culminating a 15-play, 74-yard drive. Roger Jaeger converted, cutting Iowa's lead to 17-7.

Two minutes later Neovia Greyer recovered a Hawkeye fumble at Wisconsin's 44. Eleven plays carried to Iowa's six. Then Thompson hit left tackle, cut back and raced into the end zone. Jaeger converted again, slicing Wisconsin's deficit to 17-14. Dennis Green brought the kickoff back only to Iowa's 13. The aroused Badgers stopped the Hawkeyes in three plays , forcing a punt of only 23 yards.

The fans caught fire along with the Badgers. Suddenly victory and the end of the 23-game winless streak seemed possible with 3:46 left on the clock and Wisconsin in possession at Iowa's 36. After Thompson gained one yard, Neil Graff passed 18 yards to Mel Reddick for a first down on Iowa's 17. Thompson then lost a yard and two Graff passes fell incomplete. This set up a fourth-and-11 at the 18. Graff rolled out on the next play, frantically scanned the field, spotted Randy Marks at the back of the end zone and fired. Marks grabbed the ball just before stepping over the end line. It's difficult to imagine, much less describe, the frenzied outburst that followed.

"We got the message from the (press box) spotter that Marks was wide open on the play," Coatta explained. "During the timeout we talked it over. We told Graff to have Reddick go at least 11 yards if he throws to him, but to look for Marks first. Graff did a hell of a job freeing himself, then making the play."

Graff said, "I looked across the field and saw him (Marks) stretching out and I let it go." Marks explained, "The play is designed for me to go to the corner (of the end zone). The only thing I worried about was where my foot was."

When the official raised his arms to signal touchdown, many fans learned for the first time a college receiver needed only one foot inbounds for a completion as opposed to two in pro footabll. They responded with unbridled euphoria. The Badgers added two points by trapping Green in the end zone on the ensuing kickoff for their final 23-17 margin.

Iowa tried an onside kick but Wisconsin recovered on the Hawkeye 28. After three plays gained only six yards and Jaeger's 39-yard field attempt failed, Iowa regained possession on its 20 with 1:36 left. One pass gained 34 yards to Wisconsin's 46 but Greyer intercepted the next attempt with 70 seconds to go. Graff dropped to his knee twice and time ran out. Many from the crowd of 53,714, the largest in two years, swarmed onto the field. Coatta and some of the victorious Badgers were hoisted onto the shoulders of delirious fans.

"It was one of the wildest scenes I've ever seen," said an exhausted Coatta after being dunked in the shower by his ecstatic players. "It was lovely standing there watching those seconds tick off knowing you didn't have to run another play."

Graff completed 14 of 29 passes for 159 yards. Reddick caught eight for 97 yards and Stu Voigt grabbed four for 42 yards. Thompson and Joe Dawkins ran for 107 and 72 yards, respectively.

Those Badgers won two more games that season, beating Indiana and Illinois; but they also lost four more, including a 62-7 shellacking at Ohio State. That was the school's highest losing score since Minnesota trounced the Badgers, 63-0, in 1890. Wisconsin bounced back the next week to beat Illinois, 55-14, but ended the season with a 35-10 loss at Minnesota a week later.

Coatta figured he had overseen enough of a turnaround to save his job. Hirsch thought otherwise and fired the beleaguered coach a few weeks later. Hirsch's announcement at Alumni House the night of Dec. 2 was depressing to many people who respected Coatta's intensity, integrity and devotion to the university. Later, though, he showed the same resiliency that marked him as a great quarterback 18 years earlier.

The situation was deja vu for Coatta's predecessor, Bruhn, who recalled what happened to him little more than three years earlier, Nov. 20, 1966. "You know," he said, "if I knew then what I know now, I wouldn't have been so grim about it."

Coatta, too, realized the world didn't end that night. The sun rose the next morning as usual and he went on to a more rewarding and productive life. He still had those memories of his playing days and that incredible victory over Iowa. In retrospect Coatta coached some extremely talented players that season, particularly Voigt and Dawkins, both of whom played in the National Football League later. Thompson rushed for 907 yards in 1969, a total second only to Alan Ameche's 946 in 1952, a UW record at the time. Dawkins ran for 612 yards and Graff developed into an exceptional passer.

Voigt, who led pass receivers with 39 catches, was voted most valuable player by his teammates. He still is remembered as one of the finest all-around athletes ever to attend the university, excelling in track and baseball as well as football. Actually his football career blossomed later with the Minnesota Vikings and he was selected as that NFL team's all-time tight end after he retired.

This team's record wasn't pretty but whenever Wisconsin fans discuss the great games played at Camp Randall, Iowa in '69 always ranks high among the most memorable.

Rufus Ferguson

"Rufus Ferguson was probably the most colorful athlete ever to attend the university. . . His bubbling personality and touchdown 'shuffle' became legendary."

— *Tom Butler*
Author

John Coatta surveyed empty Camp Randall Stadium in early 1969 and talked excitedly about a high school senior in Miami, Florida, named Rufus Ferguson. The coach described his young recruit as 5-6, 185 pounds and "almost impossible to knock off his feet."

"If he signs a tender and comes to Wisconsin, he'll fill this stadium," the Badger coach assured, waving an arm to emphasize the barren edifice of 78,000 that never had seen a capacity crowd.

Rufus, of course, did enroll at Wisconsin, injected new life into Badger football and capacity crowds filled the stadium for Louisiana State and Purdue games in 1971 and three more times in 1972 with the Roadrunner as the main attraction. Coatta's prophesy came true. The stadium never had been filled since the upper deck was added in 1966.

Ferguson and his touchdown "shuffle" became famous. Rufus attracted crowds like a magnet. He possessed an engaging personality. His smile and effervescence made him an instant Badger hero. Plus, his whirlwind running style enabled him to become Wisconsin's first 1,000-yard rusher. He backed up his flamboyance with deeds.

LaVern Van Dyke, a longtime UW assistant coach, once told a story about the Florida fireplug that was vintage Rufus. It happened one wintry day in 1969 when Rufus came to Madison for his official visit. The thermometer registered well below freezing and the wind chill at Truax Field made the day even more uncomfortable.

Van Dyke was assigned to greet Rufus at the airport and drive him back to the campus. Well, the 5-foot-6, 185-pound black high school senior bounced off the plane in these arctic-like conditions wearing a white Palm Beach suit and no overcoat.

"Rufus!" Van Dyke hollered. The self-styled "Roadrunner" raced over and said, "How'd ya know it was me?"

During that fall of 1969 Ferguson gained 380 yards on 64 rushing attempts in two freshman games. He also scored six touchdowns. He raced 84 yards for a touchdown in the 1970 spring intra-squad game but Coatta wasn't around to appreciate his prize recruit, having been replaced by UCLA assistant coach John Jardine the previous December.

Coatta didn't leave the cupboard bare for Jardine that 1970 season. Rufus was the catalyst but certainly not the only one who helped in the transition. Neil Graff and Larry Mialik formed an exciting passing combination. Roger Jaeger and Elbert Walker were quality offensive linemen. And, Badger fans would like to see an Alan Thompson at fullback any time.

Bill Gregory, Jim DeLisle, Chuck Winfrey, Nate Butler and Gary Buss helped spearhead the defense. Buss owned the school record for tackles for losses when he left. Gregory played 10 years in the National Football League.

Wisconsin compiled a 4-5-1 record in Jardine's first year. It was a modest improvement but attendance for home games averaged 58,223 or about 8,000 more per game than the previous year. Ferguson's totals weren't particularly imposing either but he began to show flashes of truly effective running and his personality alone excited Camp Randall crowds.

He gained 588 yards rushing in 130 carries for a 4.5 average with six touchdowns. The Badgers lost at Oklahoma, 21-7, after leading at halftime, 7-0. Ferguson gained 57 yards on 11 carries and scored the only UW touchdown on an 11-yard run. He accounted for 64 yards against Texas Christian a week later but the game ended in a 14-14 standoff.

Jardine notched his first victory in the third game at home against Joe Paterno's Penn State Nittany Lions that featured Franco Harris, Lydell Mitchell and Jack Ham. Rufus gained only 31 yards but scored a touchdown on a three-yard run. Graff and Mialik executed the big plays. Mialik streaked down the field twice for scoring passes of 68 and 52 yards, the latter with 4:33 left in the game which cemented a 29-16 victory.

The Badgers next lost to Iowa and Northwestern by identical 24-14 scores but Rufus nailed down his first 100-yard college game against the Wildcats, including a 47-yard touchdown run. The Badgers got their second victory the following week at Indiana, 30-12, as Rufus started the fireworks with a 65-yard touchdown run in the first quarter. He also scored on a one-yard run. Thompson scored twice, too, and Jaeger kicked a 34-yard field goal.

The Roadrunner struggled in successive losses to Michigan and Ohio State just as have so many of Wisconsin's finest running backs. Victories in the final two games, though, sent the Badgers into the offseason with hopes high for the future. The Illini kept Rufus off the scoreboard at Champaign but he did register his second 100-yard game (107 in 17 tries). Thompson scored twice and Mialik once on a pass from Graff covering 64 yards in a 29-17 victory.

The 39-14 victory over arch-rival Minnesota at Camp Randall gave credibility to Jardine-style football. Fans realized excitement was returning to the old stadium and optimism soared for 1971. Rufus just missed another 100-yard game (97) and he launched a 20-point fourth quarter on a trap-play up the middle that sprang him for a 29-yard touchdown run.

Ferguson enjoyed his best season in 1971 but success didn't come easy at Wisconsin and the Badgers suffered through their eighth straight losing season (4-6-1). Wisconsin beat Northern Illinois, Indiana, Michigan State and Purdue and tied Syracuse, while losing to LSU, Northwestern, Ohio State, Iowa, Illinois and Minnesota. The Badgers lost at Iowa City, 20-16, and at Minneapolis, 23-21.

The Roadrunner racked up the first 1,000-yard season in Wisconsin history, running for 1,222 yards in 249 carries for a 4.9 average. He scored 13 touchdowns. His rushing totals included 149 yards against Syracuse; 152 against Indiana with touchdown runs of 7, 19 and 40 yards; 103 against Michigan State; 136 at Ohio State; 126 at Iowa; and 211 in a losing cause at Minneapolis. He mostly ground out the yardage, his longest runs being 42, 40 and 34 yards. The loss to Minnesota was particularly depressing. Wisconsin's pass defense collapsed in the last 2 minutes, allowing the Gophers to go 80 yards in 13 plays and score with 9 seconds left.

Ferguson put the fun back into Wisconsin football and 1972, his senior season, was expected to be his best. Prospects were excellent for the first winning season in nine years. That goal seemed possible when they scored successive 31-7 victories over Northern Illinois and Syracuse with Rufus accounting for 165 and 153 yards rushing, respectively.

The Roadrunner gained only 63 yards in a 27-7 loss at LSU but he scampered for 197 when the Badgers returned home to dispatch Northwestern, 21-14. Then a pall of gloom settled over the program after losing successive games to Indiana, Michigan State and Ohio State.

The Badgers snapped their slump briefly with a 16-14 Homecoming victory over Iowa. The winning margin came with 3:42 left when Badgers Dave Schrader and Mike Seifert combined to nail Iowa tailback Dave Harris in the end zone for a safety. It was a costly victory, though, because

Ferguson suffered a severely sprained ankle that sidelined him for the next two games — losses to Purude and Illinois. That left him with 892 yards rushing heading into the final game against Minnesota at Camp Randall.

Ferguson carried the ball 36 times against the Gophers and gained 112 yards to reach 1,004 for the season in his swan song. That was the only bright spot of the day as the Gophers prevailed, 14-6, leaving the Badgers with a 4-7 mark. There were some consolations, though. After averaging 68,131 fans a game in 1971, the Badgers of '72 attracted a record 422,721 that season for the school's first 70,000 plus average in history.

Much of that could be attributed to the gate appeal of Ferguson. Coatta's prophesy of 1969 was enhanced in 1972 when a crowd of 78,723 crammed Camp Randall for the Iowa game, a school record at that time.

The Roadrunner's career totals included 2,814 yards on 594 rushing attempts with 26 touchdowns, the latter a UW record at the time.

Rufus Ferguson was probably the most colorful athlete ever to attend the university at Madison. His bubbling personality and touchdown "shuffle" became legendary. He was one of a kind. No matter how many times someone might meet Rufus during the day he would execute a variety of hip handshakes that were his specialty. His conversation was equally unique. He often outdid Ali with his prose and poetry. Following is a column I wrote for the Wisconsin State Journal Oct. 10, 1972. It describes a fictitious situation but easily could have occurred because the scenario exemplifies the Roadrunner's style and substance:

Knute Rockne was the master of locker room oratory during his glory days at Notre Dame.

Remember Pat O'Brien doing Rockne in the movies? You know, "When the going gets tough and things are going against you, go out there and win one for the Gipper."

You can buy scratchy old records of past radio highlights that feature a Rockne halftime rendition.

"Men, I want you to go out there against Army and fight. I want you to go inside and outside. Inside! Outside! Inside! Outside! I want you to fight, fight, fight. I want you to march down that field. Inside! Outside! Inside! I want you to score, score, score. I want you to win, win win."

In the background you can hear the locker room door crumble as the Fighting Irish don't bother to open it while charging out for the second half.

Well, there's a new kind of locker room oratory today. It's a kind of cool version of the old psyche job of latter day coaches. Many times coaches don't even bother. They just turn the pre-game program over to one or two of their players.

Imagine yourself a mouse in the corner of Wisconsin's quarters as John Jardine asks Rufus Ferguson for a few words before the big game.

Rufus: Yeah, baby, today we're gonna attain our goal with soul.

Chuck Richardson: Soul!

Keith Nosbusch: Wha'd he say?

Rufus: We're gonna be livin' on the rims of reality.

Richardson: The rims!

Mike Webster: Wha'd he say?

Rufus: We're going the route, baby, we're going the route with a rout. We're gonna accentuate the positive, latch onto the affirmative, and don't mess with Mr. In-Between.

Alvin Peabody: Yeah, don't mess!

Dave Lokanc: Wha'd he say?

Rufus: There ain't gonna be no slippin' or half-steppin.' We're gonna show 'em you can't kill a mosquito with an ax.

Jim Wesley: No ax!

Rufus: There's gonna be a lot of little sapphires out there waiting for the Roadrunner to do his jivin' so let's go.

Jeff Mack: Jivin', yeah!

Rufus: But, you know and I know there's no room for jivin' the Roadrunner unless my blockers become the destroyers and those big cats across the line become the destroyees.

Webster: Yeah, destroyees!

Rufus: You know and I know the Roadrunner ain't the Roadrunner unless my offensive line is in direct communication with my repertoire.

Lokanc: Yeah, repertoire!

Rufus: Are we gonna barbeque, bugaloo or mildew?

Richardson: No mildew!

Rufus: Are we gonna meditate, hesitate or castigate?

Nosbusch: Yeah, castigate!

Rufus: And, remember, when we cross the goal line, there will be no propelling the bladder against the ersatz grass or else we're liable to evoke a negative response from the man with the stripes and funny threads.

Wesley: Yeah, ersatz!

Rufus: The word for the day is mesmerize. We're gonna mesmerize the opposition with our unique effervescence.

Mack: Yeah, effervescence!

Rufus: Our flamboyancy shall not fluctuate.

Richardson: Yeah, flamboyancy!

Rufus: When I look up at that scoreboard at the end of the game I want to see that our margin of revenue is greater than our margin of cost 'cause then I'll know we've solidified our assets.

Nosbusch: Yeah, solidify!

Jardine: Wha'd he say?

Rufus did more than inject excitement into Wisconsin football. This was a period of social upheaval throughout the country. Besides anti-war protests, there was disillusionment and discontent among black students on hundreds of college campuses, including Wisconsin. Rufus Ferguson helped defuse that situation at Madison with his personality as well as his football talent. That might have been his greatest contribution to the school.

Ferguson's career statistics follow:

CollegeSTATISTICS

Rufus Ferguson

Running Back
1970 through 1972

1970

	Att.	Yds.	Avg.	TD
Oklahoma	11	57	5.2	1
TCU	21	64	3.0	0
Penn State	9	31	3.4	1
Iowa	10	18	1.8	0
Northwestern	15	107	7.1	1
Indiana	11	88	8.0	2
Michigan	7	−2	−0.3	0
Ohio State	7	21	3.0	0
Illinois	17	107	6.3	0
Minnesota	22	97	4.4	1
TOTALS	130	588	4.5	6

1971

	Att.	Yds.	Avg.	TD
Northern Illinois	16	93	5.8	2
Syracuse	26	149	5.7	2
LSU	23	97	4.2	2
Northwestern	16	46	2.9	0
Indiana	27	152	5.6	3
Michigan State	25	103	4.1	1
Ohio State	23	136	5.9	0
Iowa	28	126	4.5	2
Purdue	11	16	1.5	0
Illinois	25	93	3.7	0
Minnesota	29	211	7.3	1
TOTALS	249	1222	4.9	13

1972

	Att.	Yds.	Avg.	TD
Northern Illinois	17	165	9.7	2
Syracuse	28	153	5.5	2
LSU	17	63	3.7	0
Northwestern	34	197	5.8	2
Indiana	15	64	4.3	0
Michigan State	28	79	2.8	0
Ohio State	21	79	3.8	0
Iowa	19	92	4.8	1
Purdue	Injured - Did Not Play			
Illinois	Injured - Did Not Play			
Minnesota	36	112	3.1	0
TOTALS	215	1004	4.7	7

Career Totals

Att.	Yds.	Avg.	TD
594	2814	4.7	26

Billy Marek

"We're all out to get 1,000 for Billy. . . We're going to be immortal. Maybe nobody will remember us, but we love blocking for him."

— *Terry Stieve*
Offensive Guard

Elroy Hirsch was "Crazylegs," Alan Ameche "The Horse" and Rufus Ferguson "Roadrunner." Billy Marek was Billy Marek, a blue-collar tailback who became Wisconsin's all-time rushing and scoring leader without a nickname and with a minimum of fanfare.

Marek gained 3,709 yards rushing on 719 attempts in four years, although he carried the ball only once (against Syracuse) as a freshman in 1972. He scored 46 touchdowns, 44 rushing and one two-point conversion, for 278 points. He was second team all-American and national scoring champion in 1974, all-Big Ten twice, a two-time conference scoring leader and rushing champion in '74. Yet, he was never invited to play in any post-season all-star games, including the College All-Star classic against the NFL champions in his hometown of Chicago.

Somehow the so-called experts couldn't quite fathom Marek's brilliance. They seemed to believe this 5-8, 185-pound whippet was using mirrors to roll up all those yards. Actually he might have been the greatest escape artist since Houdini. Besides his unique talents he had the advantage of running behind such efficient offensive linemen as Mike Webster, Dennis Lick, Bob Johnson, John Reimer, Terry Stieve, Rick Koeck, Steve Lick and Joe Norwick.

One reason he probably didn't get the national notoriety he deserved was his modesty. While Rufus Ferguson would hold court around his locker after games and regale reporters with quotable one-liners, Marek popped into the shower quickly, not to avoid questions, but embarrassed about all the fuss. He usually stayed there until his skin shriveled, hoping those reporters would grow tired of waiting and leave.

Marek's three-game performance at the end of his junior season in 1974 ranks among the most remarkable in college football history. A product of Chicago's St. Rita High School, Billy rushed for 740 yards and scored 13 touchdowns against Iowa, Northwestern and Minnesota to cap his second straight 1,000-yard season. His 13 touchdowns, four each against the Hawkeyes and Wildcats and five against the Gophers, set a national record at the time.

After slithering a record 43 times through Minnesota's defense for 304 yards on a wet field in the season finale, Marek explained with characteristic modesty years later, "It was that time of the year when everything was down pat and WE were just cruising."

Marek, like Ferguson, was short with a low center of gravity. When he ran, his feet never were far off the ground. His exceptional balance made downing him without a form tackle extremely difficult. And, also like Rufus, he possessed a strong upper body.

One ironic aspect of Billy's three games in 1974 was the absence of all-American tackle Dennis Lick, who escorted Marek through enemy defenses since their years at St. Rita's. Lick didn't play a down in that stretch, having been sidelined with a knee injury.

The patched-up line, consisting of tackles Bob Johnson and John Reimer, guards Terry Stieve and Rick Koeck or Steve Lick (Dennis' brother), and center Joe Norwick, became known as "Marek's Marauders" and they pulverized the opposition in those games.

Reimer, a barrel-chested outdoorsman from Wisconsin Rapids, had the big job of replacing Dennis Lick, considered by many the greatest offensive tackle ever at Wisconsin. Although 6-3 and 262 pounds, Dennis was no awesome physical speciman who would send chills through opponents. Still, he was incredibly strong and agile, with footwork and technique offensive line coaches dream about but seldom see.

Although everyone marvelled at Marek's exploits, the little tailback himself stood in awe of Lick. As St. Rita teammates, each was named "outstanding players" in Chicago City Championship games. Marek insisted everything came easy for Dennis. "Lick beat me at tennis, ping pong, running the mile . . . everything," Marek said. "He'd be a genius, too, if he studied. He gets into a basketball game and takes it over. He's good at everything he does."

Reimer, whose wide smile belied an inner toughness, made up for his lack of Lick's finesse with determination. He possessed a perfect temperment for an offensive lineman and reveled in that role. "When you see Billy 10 or 15 yards downfield, the feeling is unbelieveable," Reimer said of his reward as an unsung lineman.

Actually, Marek's rushing totals in the first eight games in 1974 did little to foretell such an explosion. In fact, he missed the opener at Purdue, three-quarters of the Michigan game and the seventh game at Indiana because of injuries. He managed only two 100-yard games prior to the Iowa trip, gaining 123 in a 59-20 rout of Missouri and 107 during a 28-21 loss to Michigan State. He did score three touchdowns against Missouri but had only six for the season after eight games.

Then came this incredible streak during which he sparked a 28-15 victory at Iowa with 206 yards rushing, added 230 as the Badgers downed Northwestern, 52-7, and electrified a Camp Randall crowd with a record-setting 43 carries for 304 yards and five touchdowns in a 49-14 romp against Minnesota.

Ron Pollard, Ken Starch, Larry Canada and Selvie Washington carried the load in the 1974 opener at Purdue, a 28-14 victory. Marek, bothered by muscle spasms in his back all week, sat out that game. The following week Wisconsin fashioned that exciting 21-20 victory over Nebraska at Camp Randall. The 73,381 attending erupted as Jeff Mack streaked down the sidelines 77 yards for the winning touchdown after taking a pass from Gregg Bohlig.

The Badgers traveled to Colorado for their third game and struggled through a second straight three-point loss to the Buffaloes, 24-21. Marek gained 81 yards but the highlight for Wisconsin was Starch's 88-yard touchdown run. The former Madison East star zipped through the middle of the line, cut left and just outran everybody.

Starch was overshadowed by Marek in John Jardine's tailback-dominated offense, but Ken certainly ranks with the best in a long line of outstanding Wisconsin fullbacks. He probably was the fastest of them all, possessing a scintillating combination of speed and power. Plus he and Canada were exceptional blockers.

The Badgers returned home the next week to play Missouri, their third straight Big Eight opponent. That 59-20 victory might have been the high point of Jardine's eight-year tenure. His offense never executed in a more efficient manner than in the first half against the Tigers, scoring 35 points. Marek got his first 100-yard game of the season (123) and scored three touchdowns on an 81-yard run and two short plunges.

As so often was the case in Wisconsin annals, Ohio State burst the bubble the next week at Columbus, 52-7. The Badgers scored first in that game, driving 80 yards in six plays following the opening kickoff. Marek rushed for 77 of the Badgers' 324 total yards that day but Wisconsin never got into the end zone again after that first drive.

Marek suffered a leg injury in the first quarter against Michigan after gaining 42 yards on nine carries. He left the game and never returned as the Wolverines carved out a 24-20 victory. Billy didn't play at all the next week at Indiana but the Badgers won, 35-25. He returned to action against Michigan State, rushing for 107 yards and scoring twice, but the Spartans ruined Wisconsin's 67th Homecoming, 28-21, before 78,848.

Reporters witnessed a somber scene in Wisconsin's locker room afterward. The defeat left the Badgers with a 4-4 record but they lost more than a football game. Lick limped off the field after the first play of the second half with a knee injury. It was more serious than first anticipated and he underwent surgery the following Monday.

The Badgers again moved the ball impressively, outgaining the Spartans, 330 yards to 303 with 256 coming on the ground. Michigan State coach Denny Stolz said afterward, "Wisconsin has a great offensive line. No one moved the ball on us like that." But again the defense couldn't keep the opponent out of the end zone, which was a problem all that season.

Wisconsin's travel party was not the most confident group heading for Iowa and the ninth game of the season. Lick, always a comforting sight to teammates and coaches with that big No. 70 in the offensive line, was sidelined for the rest of the season. The Hawkeyes, although 3-5, always presented big problems in Kinnick Stadium.

Marek wasn't even Wisconsin's leading rusher heading into the Iowa game. Starch had 523 yards on 79 carries, 6.6 yards per try. Billy had 475 on 99 attempts and a 4.8 average. That made his Iowa performance so surprising.

Billy scored three times on runs of one, seven and 11 yards and already had gained 127 yards rushing with 5:42 left in the game. Still, the Badgers were clinging precariously to a 21-15 lead when they started their final possession on their own 21-yard line. Any mistake here could have cost them the game. What followed, though, has to be one of the most remarkable drives ever for a Wisconsin team.

Bohlig, who had developed into a cunning quarterback and an inspirational leader, handed off nine straight times to the pride of Chicago's South Side, while stunned Iowa fans looked on in disbelief. Marek managed only three yards on his first carry but then darted through the Hawkeyes in his inimitable fashion for 10, 30, 10, 6, 2, 3 and 14 before finally diving into the end zone from the one for the clinching touchdown with 78 seconds to go in the game.

Despite the outstanding performance at Iowa, Marek saw flaws in his running others didn't notice. He gained only 36 yards in the first half and said, "When I see the films, I'll see I blew the first half. I didn't do anything right. I was ad-libbing too much. I should have been following my blockers all along like I was supposed to be doing all year."

When asked why Marek carried nine straight times on the final drive, Jardine replied, "That's what was going for us." Marek added, "I was just glad to do it. I thought it was nice."

The Badgers headed for Northwestern the next week with a chance to assure themselves of a winning season. Marek boosted his season rushing total to 681 yards but with only two games left it seemed unlikely he could make the 1,000 mark for the second straight year.

But, the Badgers were on a roll and everything clicked against the Wildcats in an overwhelming 52-7 victory. Marek scored four touchdowns again on runs of six, seven and 18 yards and on a shovel pass from Bohlig that covered 10 yards. His 230 rushing yards broke a school record he set the year before against Wyoming and he did it on 29 carries.

Badger offensive linemen — Johnson, Koeck, Art Zeimetz, Norwick, Stieve and Reimer along with tight ends Jack Novak and Ron Egloff — vowed to make sure Marek gained 1,000 yards despite his injury-plagued season.

"We're all out to get 1,000 for Billy," said Stieve, one of Wisconsin's all-time premier guards who later played more than a decade for the old NFL St. Louis Cardinals. 'We're going to be immortal. Maybe nobody will remember us, but we love blocking for him."

All smiles, Marek added, "Yeah, they wanted it bad. They're always telling me they want me to get 1,000 yards. Everything was working. We started outside and then went up the middle (against Northwestern)."

Although everybody wondered what Marek could do for an encore against Minnesota, nobody figured he would top his Northwestern performance. The 89 yards he needed to hit 1,000 even seemed unlikely when that Nov. 26th dawned dark and dreary with occasional rain. This worked to Billy's advantage, however, as he scrambled for 304 yards and scored five touchdowns against the Gophers and even had a 65-yard run for an apparent touchdown nullified by a clipping penalty.

"I don't think the offensive line can take credit today," Stieve remarked on Marek's record-breaking performance. "He looked like he was doing it all on his own."

Marek's season total of 1,215 yards gave him eight more yards than he gained as a sophomore, when he had six games of 100-yards-plus, including 203 against Iowa. He enjoyed only five such games in 1974 but missed two full games and three-quarters of another because of injuries. Even more important was that the Badgers chalked up the school's first winning season (7-4) since 1963. Although cognizant of Marek's performance, his teammates realized Bohlig's exceptional leadership and voted him the team's most valuable player.

The Badgers rewarded Billy with that honor in 1975 when he set the school record with 1,281 yards, including six 100-plus games. The Badgers missed Bohlig, however, and slumped to 4-6-1 on the season.

After finishing his career with 118 yards at Minnesota in 1975, Marek left with UW single game, season and career records for rushing attempts, yards and touchdowns. Included were 13 runs of 30 or more yards, nine for touchdowns.

One humorous incident occurred prior to the start of spring practice in 1975. I wrote an off-the-wall column April 1 about how Jardine decided to switch Marek to defensive back for his senior season. The text included the most improbable premise imaginable. Not only did many readers believe it, the Madison Associated Press bureau rewrote portions and released a story on the AP wire concerning "Jardine's plan." Following is the column:

John Jardine is more than toying with the idea of switching Billy Marek to the defensive secondary next fall. The move could come at the start of spring practice Monday.

"We think Marek possesses all the attributes of a fine buck man," Jardine said last week while discussing coming spring drills.

Despite the fact that Marek led the Big Ten in rushing last fall, averaging 161 yards a game, and topped national scoring with 12.7 points per game, Jardine feels the Chicago senior's future lies in the secondary.

"He's a natural back there," Jardine commented. "Billy is short and will be able to come up quickly on runners or intended pass receivers before they realize it. Besides, just think how dangerous he will be on interceptions."

The buck man is sort of a free safety who roams the secondary and hawks the ball. Some coaches call this position the rover back. Bo Schembechler's Michigan counterpart is known as the wolf man.

Anyone who plays this position must exude confidence, hit with authority, like to tackle, and still play tough pass defense. Marek possesses all these qualifications.

Another reason for the switch is the uncertainty surrounding Steve Wagner, the Oconomowoc senior-to-be who performed there so magnificently last fall. He injured a knee in the Minnesota game and subsequently underwent surgery. His recovery is reported as "satisfactory" but nagging doubts still haunt defensive coordinator Lew Stueck.

"Wagner plays with unbelievable intensity and I'm afraid he will come back and do too much too soon," Stueck frets. "We need a backup person at that position badly and Marek fits that bill."

Although Marek gained 1,215 yards rushing in 1974 and scored 19 touchdowns, Jardine insists the move will not affect the offense measurably.

"I just wish we were as deep at all positions as we are at tailback," Jardine mused.

The coach explained that he has so many options at that position that it boggles his imagination.

It follows that Mike Morgan will move up to No. 1 tailback and operate in the same backfield with fullback Ken Starch. Morgan himself accounted for 461 yards last year as a freshman, including 50 against Minnesota, the same opponent against whom Marek romped for 304 yards in 43 carries.

"Ron Pollard can do a hell of a job at tailback, too," Jardine stressed. "Or, in a pinch we could play Starch there with Larry Canada at fullback."

It's also apparent Jardine is taking into consideration the recently recruited freshman running backs who will report to Holy Name Seminary in August — Kevin Boodry of Antigo, Kevin Cohee of Kansas City, Mo., Tim Halleran of Chicago St. Lawrence, Charles Martin of Wheaton, Ill., Ira Matthews of Rockford and Dan Relich of Wauwatosa West.

Jardine figures it's only logical that the multi-talented Marek be the one to move.

"He's quick," the coach emphasized, "and can bench press as much as most of our linemen. We'll put him on a special diet and try to beef him up to about 205 pounds by August. He'll need that extra weight during the course of a tough 11-game schedule."

Marek takes the switch philosophically, shrugging, "If it helps the team, I'll gladly move. I can't do much more than last year anyway. Let somebody else have a chance."

This seems to be an appropriate time to make the switch with Ellis Rainsberger gone and Mike Stock directing offensive backs.

Rainsberger reportedly became gravely ill about a month ago when a toothpick lodged in his intestines. Actually, the story now is the attack came after Jardine mentioned to him the possibility of switching Marek to defense.

Rainsberger, now head man at Kansas State, should recover completely today when he receives Jardine's card that reads: "April Fool!"

What so many readers missed, including the AP rewrite person, was the last line of the column. Too often readers scan and often don't complete a story. Incidently, the AP quickly put out a "kill" on its original story once somebody realized the fiction.

Others, who didn't read the complete text, bombarded Jardine's home and the UW football office with questions about the incredulous switch. Marek later chuckled over the furor with characteristic embarrassment.

Billy Marek was Billy Marek, a reluctant hero who wound up gaining more yards than "Crazylegs," "The Horse" and "Roadrunner."

Marek's career statistics follow:

College**STATISTICS**

Billy Marek

Tailback

1972 through 1975

1972

	Att.	Yds.	Avg.	TD
Syracuse	1	6	6.0	0
Varsity Reserves *(4 games)*	82	376	4.6	2

1973

	Att.	Yds.	Avg.	TD
Purdue	14	34	2.4	0
Colorado	13	75	5.8	0
Nebraska	30	145	4.8	0
Wyoming	29	226	7.8	3
Ohio State	13	49	3.8	0
Michigan	9	31	3.4	1
Indiana	33	146	4.4	3
Michigan State	13	48	3.7	0
Iowa	30	203	6.8	4
Northwestern	26	119	4.6	2
Minnesota	31	131	4.2	1
TOTALS	241	1207	5.0	14

1974

	Att.	Yds.	Avg.	TD
Purdue	Injured - Did Not Play			
Nebraska	21	45	2.1	1
Colorado	16	81	5.1	0
Missouri	13	123	9.5	3
Ohio State	16	77	4.8	0
Michigan	9	42	4.7	0
Indiana	Injured - Did Not Play			
Michigan State	24	107	4.5	2
Iowa	34	206	6.1	4
Northwestern	29	230	7.9	4
Minnesota	43	304	7.1	5
TOTALS	205	1215	5.9	19

1975

	Att.	Yds.	Avg.	TD
Michigan	21	58	2.8	0
South Dakota	12	93	7.8	3
Missouri	31	117	3.8	2
Kansas	19	77	4.1	1
Purdue	25	152	6.1	1
Ohio State	12	38	3.2	0
Northwestern	36	198	5.5	2
Illinois	39	189	4.9	2
Iowa	17	59	3.5	1
Indiana	31	182	5.9	1
Minnesota	29	118	4.1	0
TOTALS	272	1281	4.7	13

The All-Stars

"I remember getting off the bus at Soldier Field and saying, 'What the hell are we doing here?' "

— Pat Richter
Wide Reciever

During the 42 years from 1934 to '76, the sports world considered Chicago's College All-Star game the unofficial start of every football season.

The collegiate senior all-stars played the National Football League champions in those games and won only nine of the 41 and a fraction contests during that span. In three of these nine, University of Wisconsin stars were named most valuable players of the game — Pat Harder in 1943, Elroy "Crazylegs" Hirsch in '46 and Ron VanderKelen in '63.

The reason for the "41 and a fraction games" was that the '74 game was cancelled because of the NFL players strike and the final game in '76 was halted with 1 minute 22 seconds left in the third quarter and the Pittsburgh Steelers leading the All-Stars 24-0. A torrential rainstorm struck Soldier Field and thousands of youngsters poured onto the field and tore down both goalposts.

Many other fans followed and were diving onto the slick artificial turf, sliding 20 to 30 yards. Ushers and security police were unable to clear fans from the flooded field and after 12 minutes officials called the game.

Arch Ward, the late sports editor of the Chicago Tribune, originated the idea of the College All-Star game in 1934, a year following his successful venture with baseball's "summer classic" that pitted the National League All-Stars against their American League counterparts in conjunction with Chicago's World's Fair.

One has to wonder now how the game's popularity grew considering the first one, featuring the Chicago Bears, ended in a scoreless tie. The Bears won the next year, 5-0, and the Stars and Detroit Lions were deadlocked, 7-7, at the end of the third contest. But those games and baseball's classics were the "spectaculars" of that bygone era. There wasn't any television then and watching the big football names of the day in the same arena was a happening.

Now we see games every weekend and several nights during the week. Television is saturated with football and other sporting events since the advent of cable. Back in 1941 there was something special about having Michigan's Tom Harmon, Minnesota's George Franck, Boston College's Charlie O'Rourke and UCLA's Jackie Robinson, later of Brooklyn Dodgers fame, playing on the same team against the Bears with Sid Luckman and George McAfee.

The pro game hadn't advanced very far out of the bush leagues back in the '30s and the collegians led the series after the first five games with two victories, one loss and two ties. Sammy Baugh of TCU and his college teammates beat the Green Bay Packers, 6-0, in '37 and the Cecil Isbell-led stars whipped the Washington Redskins, 28-16, the next year. Those two quarterbacks were instrumental in boosting the pro game during the next few years.

Eventually the pros dominated. Their game became too sophisticated for the college teams, which practiced together for about two weeks. The final tally showed the pros winning 31 games and the All-Stars nine with two ties.

The pros won the last 12 games after the All-Stars, with Wisconsin's VanderKelen and Pat Richter combining on a 73-yard pass-run for the winning touchdown, beat the Packers, 20-17, in 1963. Some years later Richter recalled, "I remember getting off the bus at Soldier Field and saying, 'What the hell are we doing here?' I think the Packers took us lightly. We got the jump on them.

"Actually, the play that beat them was called a 'Packer pass,' designed for a five-yard gain," Pat added. "It turned out to be the longest I ever had, college or pro."

The Packers returned in 1966, '67 and '68 to swamp the collegians. After the '66 victory, 38-0, former Packer great Willie Davis said, "There were 16 of us in that 1963 game and it was boiling in our minds. We wanted this one."

Harder played the key role in the All-Stars' 27-7 win over the Redskins in 1943 when the game was moved from Soldier Field to Northwestern's Dyche Stadium during World War II. Stationed in the Navy at Great Lakes then, I saw that game and Harder punctuated his all-American stature of the previous fall. He scored on a 37-yard pass from Tulsa's Glenn Dobbs and a 33-yard run from scrimmage. He also kicked two conversions.

The country and the sports world were getting back to normal following the war in '46 when Hirsch spearheaded the All-Stars' 16-0 victory over the Los Angeles Rams. Five years later Hirsch was instrumental in the Rams winning their only NFL championship.

Elroy set an all-time All-Star record with a 68-yard touchdown run from scrimmage in the '46 game and also scored on a 62-yard pass from another future Hall of Famer, Otto Graham of Northwestern and the Cleveland Browns. Harder, like Hirsch, just out of the Marines, returned for an encore and kicked conversions after each touchdown. Hirsch's touchdown reception was even more spectacular than his scoring run. He caught the ball over his head on the dead run. It was a portent of things to come later at Los Angeles.

The All-Stars beat the Bears, 16-0, in '47; the Philadelphia Eagles, 17-7, in '50; the Browns, 30-27, in '55; and the Lions, 35-19, in '58. It seemed as if the latter victory was the last hurrah for the collegians as the Baltimore Colts won in '59 and '60, the Eagles in '61 and the Packers in '62. Then came VanderKelen and Richter.

The All-Stars were clinging to a precarious 13-10 lead in the fourth quarter when they took possession on their own 20-yard line. On third down from the 27 VanderKelen flipped a short pass to Richter, who spun away from Jesse Whittenton and raced for the clinching touchdown. The Packers scored again later but the three-point margin held up.

VanderKelen set up an earlier touchdown with a 21-yard toss to Richter and clinched the game's most valuable player award with those two clutch plays and 141 yards on nine completions in 11 passing attempts.

Graham, who coached the All-Stars to that victory, said after the game, "I'll tell you how we won. We had a quarterback (VanderKelen) who memorized the game plan and carried it out to the letter."

Fifteen of the 34 UW players invited to the All-Star game over the years contributed to victories. Tackle John Golemgeske and fullback Ed Jankowski played in 1937; Harder, fullback Len Calligaro and quarterbacks Bob Diercks and Tom Farris in '43; Harder, Hirsch, tackle George Hekkers, end Jack Mead and guard Evan Vogds in '46; center Fred Negus and tackle Clarence Esser in '47; fullback Alan Ameche and end Jim Temp in '55; and Richter and VanderKelen in '63.

Defensive back Steve Wagner and tackle Dennis Lick played in the rain-shortened last game and center Mike Webster was invited to the ill-fated '74 contest that never materialized.

Other Badgers selected to play with the All-Stars were guard Lynn Hovland and fullback Howie Weiss in '39; fullback George Paskvan, '41; quarterback Farris also in '42; tackle Frank Lopp in '45; halfbacks Jug Girard and Earl Maves in '48; fullback Ben Bendrick in '49; linebacker Hal Faverty and end Pat O'Donahue in '52; quarterback Jim Haluska and guard John Dittrich in '56; guard Jerry Stalcup in '60; center Ken Bowman and tackle Roger Pillath in '64; and tackle Bill Gregory in '71.

Hirsch said his introduction in Soldier Field that night in '46 gave him one of his biggest thrills in sports.

"They turn out all the lights," he explained, "and have two spotlights on you while you're running up the field. They also have a spotlight on a huge American flag down on one end and they play your school song. Boy, that really got me."

Those games raised millions of dollars for Chicago Tribune charities but they went the way of the dinosaur with the advent of expanded pro football seasons, huge contracts, television extravaganzas, Super Bowls, sensationalized Olympics and a plethora of college bowl games.

Crowds of 90,000 and 100,000 in the '40s and '50s dwindled to 50,000 during the last decade and the prestige of the once-popular game with them.

Mike Kalasmiki

"Imbued with a free spirit, Mike occasionally delighted in trying to throw a football literally out of Camp Randall."

— *Tom Butler*
Author

John Jardine's 1975, '76 and '77 teams did not measure up to the '74 outfit and the decline took its toll on the coach, although fan interest never waned. In fact, his last team drew an average of 72,682 for six home games.

Following the 4-6-1 of Marek's final year in '75, the Badgers registered back-to-back 5-6 marks the next two years. The '77 season was particularly disconcerting because the Badgers sported a 5-0 record heading to Michigan for game six. About a dozen bowl representatives crowded the press box, each one adorned in a distinctive blazer. The Badgers took the field with hopes high.

The euphoria faded like a wisp of smoke in a windstorm as the Wolverines proceeded to run roughshod through the Badgers on the way to a 56-0 victory. Wisconsin then proceeded to lose five more games, including two additional shutouts. The strain and frustration racked Jardine physically. He decided enough was enough and resigned. There was no internal pressure and only a smattering of alumni discontent.

This sent the athletic board scurrying for a new coach once more and the university settled on Dave McClain, who had compiled an impressive record while guiding Ball State in the Mid-American Conference.

McClain's arrival in Decmeber of 1977, of course, signalled another rebuilding project and quest for a "turnaround," the third such campaign at Wisconsin in 12 years. Lack of continuity became an albatros around the neck of Wisconsin football and "turnaround" as much a part of McClain's lexicon as "throw game."

Although the new coach espoused option football, his principal offensive weapon in 1978 was a 6-4, 215-pound quarterback named Mike Kalasmiki. The Addison, Ill., dropback passer possessed a howitzer-like right arm but not a great deal of agility. Imbued with a free spirit, Mike occasionally delighted in trying to throw a football literally out of Camp Randall. It provided a challenge. He wasn't showing off. He'd hurl the pigskin toward the rim of the stadium whether anyone was watching or not.

Freshman quarterback John Josten, one of McClain's first recruits, started the season opener against Richmond, mainly because he could run the option. He did throw five passes and completed just one, but that toss to David Charles covered 80 yards for a touchdown, tying a school record set originally in 1919. Eventually the Badgers eked out a 7-6 victory.

A 28-7 victory at Northwestern in the second game was fashioned around the running of Ira Matthews and Tom Stauss who rushed for 125 and 123 yards, respectively.

Kalasmiki, who bided his time for two years behind Anthony Dudley and Charles Green, didn't make his season debut until the third game against Oregon.

He was relegated to No. 3 quarterback behind Josten and Green. That wasn't surprising. The year before Mike injured a knee severely when he fell while doing some extra throwing after practice. Coaches feared he might never play football again.

Following a long rehabilitation, Kalasmiki arrived at preseason practice with considerable confidence but not much interest from the coaching staff. His chance came when Josten injured a knee in the first quarter against Oregon. But Mike, no stranger to freak accidents, almost wasn't ready even then. The previous Tuesday after practice he reportedly stumbled on the fire escape that served as the rear entrance to his State Street apartment. "I tried to grab the rail when I fell but I missed it," Mike explained. Besides sporting two black eyes and 11 stitches across the top of his nose, he needed ice packs each morning to open his left eye.

Kalasmiki shook off that injury and led the Badgers to a 22-19 victory over the Ducks at Camp Randall, completing 16 of 35 passes for 232 yards and a pair of touchdowns, one to Charles for 26 yards and another to Tim Stracka for 12. The Badgers rallied from a 19-7 deficit and scored all of their points in the fourth quarter.

Kalasmiki later fretted about his lowly position on the depth chart, saying, "I wondered about that. I felt I had to wait for my shot. But I knew I could throw the ball. I had confidence in myself."

Wisconsin trounced Indiana, 34-7, the next week on the strength of three touchdowns by Ira Matthews, including a 71-yard punt return; and a week later fought to a 20-20 tie at Illinois. So, the Badgers charged into the sixth game against Michigan at Camp Randall with a 4-0-1 record.

A familiar pattern followed. Losses to the Wolverines, Michigan State and Ohio State by overwhelming margins knocked the Badgers back into Big Ten reality. A 24-24 standoff with Purdue at Madison braked the slide just temporarily because the Badgers lost at Iowa, 38-24, a week after the Purdue game. Boilermaker quarterback Mark Herrmann racked up all the statistics but Kalasmiki grabbed the headlines by throwing for all three Wisconsin touchdowns and a two-point conversion that tied the game in the last 25 seconds.

McClain called the later debacle at Iowa "the most disappointing loss I've ever been associated with." He added the biting remark, "We had some guys who tossed it in today." The defeat left the Badgers with a 4-4-2 record heading into the finale against Minnesota and hopes for a winning season were fading.

The Badgers earned redemption for their horrendous performance at Iowa by stuffing Minnesota, 48-10. The temperature never rose above 35 degrees at Camp Randall but the Badgers burned the Gophers for 34 points in the second half and registered the school's first winning football season since 1974 and only the second in 15 years.

Led by Matthews, no group of Wisconsin seniors ever bowed out with a more satisfying performance. The Rockford, Ill., tailback rushed for 134 yards and scored three touchdowns on a 31-yard run from scrimmage, a 34-yard pass from Kalasmiki and a 64-yard punt return.

"I remember Larry Canada's last game when I was a sophomore," Matthews said. "He got a lot of yards, almost 1,000 for the season, and I remember how happy he was. This being my last game I wanted to do well. The last game is the one you remember. It probably was my best game."

Stauss enjoyed a spectacular day also, gaining 113 yards rushing on only eight carries for a 14.1 average. Included was a 73-yard touchdown run. He also scored on a nine-yard pass from Kalasmiki.

Even with this exceptional running by Matthews and Stauss, Minnesota coach Cal Stoll said, "Sure I'm surprised Wisconsin ran so easily. We don't discount any facet of any team's offense, but we knew we had to stop them from throwing. That's what they do best and you have to stop what a team does best. Their quarterback (Kalasmiki) is the guy who pulled off the big plays — both running and passing."

And, Kalasmiki did complete 13 of 26 passes for 173 yards and three touchdowns as the Badgers rolled up 500 total yards. He boosted his total of touchdown passes to 10 in the Big Ten, tying a school record set by Ron VanderKelen in 1962. Mike finished the season with 107 completions in 231 attempts for 1,378 yards and 12 touchdowns. He also ran for

169 yards and was voted the team's most valuable player.

A final game like the one in 1978 leaves a sweet taste in the mouths of players and an aura of optimism surrounding the program. Fan interest mounted heading into 1979 but that season was cloaked in misfortune from the start. First, freshman defensive back Jay Seiler of Schofield suffered a head injury in spring practice and died a week later. The following July wide receiver Wayne Souza of New Bedford, Mass., who caught the two-point conversion pass that tied Purdue in '78, drowned in Lake Monona in a boating mishap.

Naturally the players were devastated by these two fatalities. There is a tendency for young people to think they're immortal and the loss of these two spirited teammates preyed on the minds of players and coaches alike. The Badgers appeared to be sleep-walking through preseason practice.

The Badgers lost their opener at Purdue, 41-20, and then blanked a weak Air Force Academy team, 38-0, at home. McClain experienced many of the frustrations of his predecessor during succeeding weeks when the Badgers lost six of the next seven games, including staggering shutouts by Ohio State, 59-0, and Michigan, 54-0. The one bright spot was the progress of freshman nose guard Tim Krumrie of Mondovi. Defensive coordinator Jim Hilles discovered early young Krumrie was made of the right stuff.

Lack of continuity at quarterback was a principal drawback for Wisconsin that season. Kalasmiki suffered a knee injury at Purdue and hobbled for a while. Josten broke the tibia just above his right ankle in the same opening game and was sidelined for the season. This left Steve Parish and Kevin Motl sharing quarterback duties.

Then Kalasmiki fractured his right thumb in practice prior to the San Diego State game, so Motl got the starting call there. Mike returned to action against Iowa and started the next week at Michigan but didn't perform at 100 percent efficiency.

Wisconsin took a 2-7 record into the final home game at Camp Randall against Northwestern. Morale sagged noticeably after the Michigan trip. Still 68,229 showed up to watch the Wildcats and Badgers. Kalasmiki reached the level of his junior season while sparking a 28-3 victory. He completed 17 of 23 passes for 265 yards and two touchdowns, scoring himself on a sneak.

The Badgers got a lift from that Northwestern victory but many people figured the Minnesota game meant nothing more than that the season was mercifully coming to an end. The players didn't think that way, though. They remembered how satisfying the victory over Minnesota was for the seniors the year before and were determined to salvage the same kind of "high" for Kalasmiki's class.

That seemed unlikely, however, when the Gophers raced to a 14-0 lead in the first 7½ minutes of the game. Undaunted, the Badgers rallied with two quick touchdowns that Kalasmiki scored on runs of 28 and four yards.

About this time, with the score tied at 14-all, one Minnesota wag in the press box stood up and proclaimed with derision, "If Minnesota gets beat by this horse-bleep outfit, they ought to quit."

Shortly after that remark Kalasmiki flipped a screen pass to Troy King in the right flat. The freshman tailback from Freeport, Ill., broke loose with key blocks from Ray Snell and guard Jim Martine and raced 53 yards for a touchdown. Steve Veith's conversion gave the Badgers a 21-14 lead and they never trailed again.

The Badgers eventually increased their margin to 42-24, but had to beat back a late Minnesota rally before walking off the Memorial Stadium field with a 42-37 victory. By that time the perpetrator of the aforementioned disparagement had departed. Remaining reporters never did hear his final assessment of the proceedings.

Kalasmiki's swan song produced 13 completions in 26 attempts for 252 yards and two touchdowns. He also ran 11 times for 72 yards, a 6.6 average, and scored three times. It was a memorable finish to his rollercoaster season.

Mike's season totals didn't approach those of his junior year, mainly because injuries reduced his playing time. Snell and fullback Dave Mohapp, who led Wisconsin rushers with 603 yards, earned all-Big Ten honors, while Tom Stauss, the leading pass receiver with 38 catches, was voted Wisconsin's most valuable player.

The manner in which Kalasmiki rallied his forces for victories in the last two games that season enhanced his reputation as a winner. Although the losing season disappointed McClain in his second year at the helm, progress was evident and the returning nucleus boded well for the future.

Kalasmiki is remembered as a guy who held things together during the transition from Jardine to McClain and through the tragedies that overshadowed the 1979 season. He did not accomplish this alone, of course, but his leadership and fortitude eased the situation, assuring him a niche in UW football lore.

Jess Cole

"Really, a lot of it is just instinct. You don't think about it. You just go out and do it."

— Jess Cole
Quarterback

If Tim Krumrie wasn't enough, Mondovi, a town of 2,400 in Buffalo County, sent another talented football player to the University of Wisconsin during the Dave McClain era. Jess Cole, a 6-2, 195-pound freshman, was at the helm in 1981 when Wisconsin defeated Michigan, Purdue and Ohio State in the same season for the first time in history.

Cole, a much-heralded high school athlete, arrived at Madison a year after his former teammate, Krumrie, who already was rolling up incredible defensive numbers and stamping himself as one of the best ever at Wisconsin. But Cole was used sparingly during most of the 1980 season while playing behind John Josten.

The husky towhead got his big chance in the 10th game at Northwestern when Josten aggravated his ailing left leg. The Badgers led by an improbable 8-7 score at the time by virtue of two Mark Doran field goals and a safety. Cole directed Wisconsin on a 59-yard touchdown drive in his first series. His 14-yard scramble to the Wildcat one set up Troy King's touchdown. Cole passed two yards to Craig Fredrick for another touchdown and a 22-7 lead at halftime.

The eventual 39-19 victory was important because it snapped a three-game losing streak and demonstrated a diversified attack spearheaded by Cole, John Williams, Thad McFadden and Dave Mohapp. "I thought Jess Cole did a darn fine job," McClain beamed afterward. "He showed a lot of poise, especially on those screens when they were blitzing. That was a great pass he threw to Craig (Fredrick) just before halftime. That was the turning point of the game."

Cole got his first start against Minnesota in the final game of the season. Deer hunters tramped the north woods and only 54,229 fans showed up on that sunny, 55-degree Nov. 22nd. Cole took advantage of the opportunity as few freshmen ever do, especially quarterbacks. He spearheaded a 25-7 victory, scoring all four Wisconsin touchdowns on a 52-yard run and three one-yard sneaks. He ran for 92 yards on 15 carries and had to pass only seven times, completing five for 57 yards.

His long touchdown run epitomized classic option football and actually cracked the Gopher defense. Minnesota led at the time, 7-6, and Cole's score with 3:08 left in the third quarter shook the offense out of its doldrums and the Badgers added two more touchdowns in the fourth period.

Much credit also must go to the defense, which shackled the Gophers most of the way, limiting them to 111 yards on the ground. Krumrie was credited with 17 tackles, including 10 solos, and Dave Ahrens, the team's most valuable player that year, had 12 stops.

But, back to Cole's long run. Tailback King deserved a big assist when Cole faked a handoff to him. Much of the defensive flow followed King as Jess bootlegged toward the east sideline. Cole outmaneuvered the remaining Gophers with some nifty footwork as he sped for the end zone.

"Early in the week we didn't run that play right," King explained. "Then we put more time into that fake. I just fell into it from practicing. I went down about 10 yards and a couple guys (Gophers) grabbed me but let go and I saw him (Cole) running down the sidelines."

Cole didn't remember much about his dazzling effort but said, "Really, a lot of it is just instinct. You don't think about it. You just go out and do it. I'm just glad it worked."

Although Cole did show good instincts as a runner, skeptics questioned his speed and Jess admitted, "I'm not very fast, about 4.9 (seconds in the 40). But I was fast enough today, wasn't I?"

McClain presented a pleased but cautious assessment of Cole's performance. Some Badger faithful were concerned that he didn't recruit a passing quarterback more vigorously. Many favored someone like Illinois' David Wilson or Purdue's Mark Herrmann. McClain, though, intimated a preference for a combination dropback and rollout passer.

"I thought his performance was outstanding," the coach said of Cole. "But I've seen it coming. We've always felt that he was going to come along. But, one game doesn't make a season," he cautioned.

There was an ominous tone for Cole in the wavering attitude on the part of McClain and the offensive coaching staff. This preference for the "throw game" didn't manifest itself until late in the 1981 season. It probably shocked Cole most of all.

Although the final two victories salvaged something of the '80 season, the second straight 4-7 record showed things hadn't changed much around Camp Randall and no "turnaround" appeared imminent.

The attitude of Wisconsin fans heading into the 1981 season could be described best with the old saw, "cautiously optimistic." They had seen the bubble burst too many times in the past and with Michigan, the preseason No. 1 pick in the polls, coming to Madison for the opener, confidence in the Badgers wavered.

The uncertainty was evident when 68,733 showed up to watch the mighty Wolverines in a stadium that held 78,000. There was no mad rush for tickets even on a balmy September day. Those 68,733 were rewarded though, with one of the most memorable Wisconsin performances ever witnessed in the venerable old arena.

Those Badgers shocked the football world by dismantling Michigan, 21-14. The final score didn't reflect the domination exhibited by the Badgers in their first victory over Michigan since 1962. Wisconsin executed 78 offensive plays to Michigan's 53, rolled up a first-down advantage of 23-8 and outgained the Wolverines in total yards, 439 to 229.

It also was only Wisconsin's second victory over a Michigan team in Madison, the other being a 16-13 decision in 1960. It also snapped a 14-game mastery the Wolverines held over the Badgers.

Michigan scored first on quarterback Steve Smith's four-yard run in the second quarter for a 7-0 lead. The Badgers matched that on Cole's 17-yard scoring pass to Marvin Neal and then added another on Chucky Davis' one-yard plunge with two seconds left in the first half for a 14-7 edge.

The Wolverines tied the score with 9:16 left in the third quarter when Butch Woolfolk raced 89 yards for a touchdown. Take away that run and the Michigan offense showed only 140 total yards all afternoon. This run didn't faze the Badgers, however, because they came back in their next series with the winning touchdown and the most electrifying play of the season.

Starting on their own 19, the Badgers overcame a holding penalty and finally managed an automatic first down when the Wolverines held McFadden on a passing situation. With third-and-nine at the 29, Cole flipped a screen pass out of the shotgun formation to John Williams, a speedy tailback from Muskegon, Mich. He raced down the west sideline behind a cordon of blockers for the touchdown as fans errupted into an uncontrollable frenzy. He outran the remaining Michigan defenders after getting a crunching block from Neal.

"After those first three guys threw those blocks (Carlton Walker, Bob Winckler and Ron Versnik), it was really good," Williams said. "I sprinted up the field and had a lineman in front of me. I was weaving back and forth from his (Neal's) left shoulder to his right to see how the block was gonna come out. I cut back up to the inside and two other guys started after me. Marvin just cleaned 'em up for me."

A smiling Neal explained, "I sacrificed my body. I just laid my body out there and tried to get as many as I could. I got two or three, I don't know."

The rest was left to the defense. Neither team scored in the fourth quarter. You don't make all-American in one game but Krumrie and Matt Vanden Boom attracted enough attention against Michigan to keep voters focused on their exploits the rest of the season.

Krumrie again led the defense with 13 tackles, six unassisted. Vanden Boom picked off three Smith passes, killing three of Michigan's last six possessions with interceptions.

Krumrie summed up the victory by saying, "I was really fired up and after the first series everybody had a sparkle in their eyes when we came off. I knew the next series we were gonna do the same thing."

Mohapp rushed for 87 yards and Davis got 69. Most of Davis' yards came in key situations to keep drives alive and the media voted him player of the game. Cole rushed for 41 yards on 11 tries and completed eight of 17 passes for 182 yards and two touchdowns.

Cole wasn't born when Wisconsin beat Michigan the only other time in Madison and he admitted, "When I sit down and talk with my dad, that's when I'll appreciate the victory."

The Wisconsin State Journal sports page the next day featured a streamer across the top that proclaimed, "Dream comes true." Everybody understood. It also included a color picture of huge fullback Gerald Green and McClain embracing in sheer ecstacy. A copy of that page, with its exhilarating moment frozen in time, hung in the coach's office until the day he died.

UCLA knocked Wisconsin partisans back to earth the next week at Camp Randall by manhandling the Badgers, 31-13. The Badgers then reeled off victories over Western Michigan, Purdue and Ohio State. The latter started an unprecedented run of four victories over the Buckeyes in five years.

The margin in the 24-21 decision over Ohio State came on a 50-yard field goal by Wendell Gladem as time ran out in the first half. It sent the Badgers off the field with a 17-14 lead. Seldom has Camp Randall witnessed the crowd explosion that occurred after Wisconsin scored 11 points in the last 24 seconds of the half.

It all started when Al Seamonson recovered Buckeye Jeff Cisco's fumble at the Ohio State 29 with 24 seconds on the clock. The Buckeyes were offside on the first play and then Cole passed to Neal for a touchdown and Williams bolted into the end zone for a two-point conversion.

On Ohio State's first play after the ensuing kickoff Tim Spencer fumbled Art Schlichter's pitchout and David Greenwood recovered on the Buckeye 33 with 8 seconds left. Cole's first down pass misfired and Gladem then performed his heroics.

As Wisconsin fans quickly discovered, even victories over Michigan, Purdue and Ohio State do not a season make. Following the Ohio State excitement, the Badgers lost successive games to Michigan State, 33-14, and Illinois, 23-21. Even during the four straight seven-win seasons under McClain the Badgers didn't contain their emotions well or handle success with aplumb. After the Michigan State loss the puzzled coach shrugged, "I don't think there's much question, Michigan State came to play and we came to watch and that's exactly what happened."

Cole struggled through his worst game as a Badger at Michigan State. Randy Wright replaced him in the fourth quarter and led the Badgers on their only scoring drive of the game, passing three yards to Jeff Nault for the touchdown. This was a portent of things to come.

Wisconsin got back on track with a 52-0 bludgeoning of Northwestern and a 28-7 victory at Indiana that left the Badgers in a tie with Michigan for the Big Ten lead. Both had 5-2 conference records. Cole passed for two touchdowns and ran for another against the Hoosiers.

The Badgers were upbeat heading into their 10th game, a showdown with Iowa before a sellout throng of 78,731 at Camp Randall. But, the Hawkeyes jumped to a 17-0 first half lead and then let their defense take charge in a 17-7 victory. Wisconsin's touchdown came on Cole's pass to McFadden covering 52 yards. Otherwise Jess struggled through a frustrating afternoon, throwing three interceptions.

Wisconsin salvaged a 26-21 victory at Minnesota in the finale on some late heroics by Wright. The Badgers wound up with a 7-4 record, the school's best since 1974, and were invited to the Garden State Bowl in the Meadowlands of New Jersey, where they lost a hard-fought battle with Tennessee, 28-21.

Krumrie and Vanden Boom made first team all-American and Greenwood landed a second-team berth. Dave Levenick, a quality linebacker who performed yeoman service with little fanfare, was voted the team's most valuable player.

Iowa tied Ohio State for the Big Ten championship with 6-2 records and Hayden Fry lost his first Rose Bowl appearance, 28-0, to Washington. Wisconsin shared third place with Michigan and Illinois on 6-3 records. It's obvious where the Badgers would have spent New Year's Day had they managed just one more victory.

It became obvious which direction the Wisconsin program was heading when Wright took over the controls in the second half against Tennessee. Wright became No. 1 at the start of the '82 season and took every snap in the first three games. Cole decided he would rather play regularly in the

Wisconsin State University Conference than languish on the sidelines in the Big Ten. He dropped out of school and transferred to the UW-Eau Claire. He found contentment with the Blugolds and led them to the 1983 WSUC championship.

Cole became yesterday's hero on the Madison campus. Some criticized him for not being a team player. They thought he should ride out his disappointment and contribute, if in no other way than providing depth. Others sympathized with a young man who didn't want to see his youth slip away in those few precious college years without exhibiting his talents on the gridiron.

No mater what the opinion, or whether Cole harbored deep resentment, he was there in the thick of some of Wisconsin's most exciting victories and those memories linger.

The Wright Stuff

"If I had stayed at Notre Dame and they won the national championship, it wouldn't have meant as much as when we won the first bowl game for Wisconsin."

— *Randy Wright*
Quarterback

Randy Wright came to epitomize Wisconsin football of the early 1980s — fun, excitement, a rollercoaster of emotions and enough victories to keep fans streaming into Camp Randall. This was the heyday of the UW band's "fifth quarter."

Wright engineered the most thrilling successses during that period, including victories over Minnesota, 26-21, in '81; Purdue, 35-31, and Ohio State, 6-0, in '82; and Missouri, 21-20, and the Boilermakers, 42-38, in '83. He also led the Badgers to their only post-season victory, a 14-3 triumph over Kansas State at the '82 Independence Bowl.

The Wright family lived in St. Charles, Ill., when Randy was recruited by Notre Dame, where he spent his freshman year in 1979. He didn't find fulfillment with the Fighting Irish and remembered his previous contact with Wisconsin coaches, who pursued him vigorously out of high school. He decided to transfer and sat out the 1980 season under NCAA rules.

Wright spent the 1981 season behind Jess Cole on the depth chart and didn't get his big break until 1:54 remained in the Minnesota game with the Badgers trailing, 21-20. He replaced Cole and guided the Badgers 85 yards in six plays for the winning touchdown. Passes to end Michael Jones for 17 and 49 yards and to Craig Fredrick for nine carried to Minnesota's 10. Troy King gained three yards and Wright hit Jones in the end zone for the score. It clinched a Garden State Bowl bid.

Possibly the excitement of the school's first bowl appearance in 19 years spooked the Badgers and they lost to Tennessee in Giants Stadium at the Meadowlands. Wright replaced Cole at the start of the second half and passed for two touchdowns but the Volunteers prevailed, 28-21. It became obvious, though, Randy would start spring practice as No. 1 quarterback.

Ironically, two of the three games Wright remembered most vividly were losses to Illinois, 29-28, and Indiana, 20-17, in 1982. The other was the 6-0 victory at Ohio State the same year.

"It was that Illinois game where we threw the bounce pass," Randy said. "That is what I thought college football was all about. You had two good teams, a TV audience and a very enthusiastic sellout crowd. It was a beautiful, crisp fall day and you had an absolutely nail-biting game right down to the very wire; right to where (Tony) Eason brings them back and they kick a field goal right at the very end."

The "bounce pass" was uncharacteristic of the usually conservative McClain. I first saw the play executed by one of Dick Rundle's teams at Monona Grove High School and McClain resurrected it at just the right moment.

Illinois was leading at the time, 26-22. With second-and-10 at the Illini 40, Wright flipped a long lateral to Al Toon in the left flat. The ball fell short but skidded off the artificial turf into Toon's hands. The split end shrugged as if it was an incomplete pass. The Illini defense relaxed. Al then lofted a pass to a wide-open Jeff Nault, who ran into the end zone. Shockingly Wendell Gladem's extra-point try hit the left upright and fell harmlessly to the ground, leaving the Badgers with a two-point lead and inviting disaster.

That's exactly what happened. Eason directed Illinois 51 yards in the last 52 seconds, enabling Mike Bass to kick a 46-yard field goal with time running out.

Wright was knocked unconscious in the second quarter of the Indiana game two weeks later, also at Camp Randall. An ambulance drove onto the field and sped Randy to University Hospital. He made a dramatic reentrance at the start of the fourth quarter and led the Badgers back in front. But again they were thwarted by a field goal, this time with 4 seconds left.

The Ohio State game earlier that season proved to be the most significant in McClain's eight years as coach because it was Wisconsin's first victory at Columbus since 1918. The Badgers scored in the first quarter, then held off the Buckeyes with a drive that consumed the last 8 minutes, 33 seconds of the game. It included 17 straight running plays and six first downs to Ohio State's 10. The longest run was Wright's 10-yard dash around right end on the 12th play.

The drive almost ended when John Williams fumbled on the 14th play at the Buckeye 15. Fortunately for the Badgers, tackle Bob Winckler spotted the loose football and pulled it to safety under his chest.

Rain poured down on Ohio Stadium when Brad Grabow recovered a Buckeye fumble at Wisconsin's 21-yard line with 8:33 left, halting what seemed certain to be the deciding touchdown drive.

Even then, few expected Wisconsin could control the football the rest of the way. The Badgers started in a precarious position, not only because of where they were on the field, but because Wright tore ligaments in his right thumb when he was tackled during the previous series. He also sustained a hip-pointer earlier in the game.

"I remember stepping in the huddle and telling our linemen I couldn't throw the ball," Wright said. "I told (Ron) Versnik and Winckler and (Mark) Subach and that whole group, 'If you guys don't do the job, we're going to wind up punting the ball.'

"And there were holes galore. We just ran the ball well and it was fortunate because we had a lot of three yards and a cloud of dust (or splash of water). We didn't have a 40-yard run, which probably would have hurt us. We used three plays and got another first down, which takes another 2 minutes off the clock.

"Everybody could take pride in that because it was an ultimate team victory. The defense shut them out and the offense scored all it needed."

Williams accounted for four of the six first downs in the drive. Two came on fourth-down plays.

McClain remembered that he and many of his Badgers stood in that same locker room three years earlier after absorbing a 59-0 shellacking at the hands of the Buckeyes. "We never once mentioned that all week long. Each guy, if he's got any memory at all, remembers three years ago."

Krumrie remembered, but he wasn't at all intimidated this time in the huge horseshoe. "It was a horrible feeling when I was down here as a freshman. I've never been beat that bad before in my life and never hope to be again."

The State Journal's front page the next day contrasted those two occurances. A black and white L. Roger Turner picture of McClain and his players walking off the field in '79 with the 59-0 scoreboard in the background was situated on the left side of the page. A color shot by the late J.D. Patrick with linebacker Kyle Borland walking under the same scoreboard, this time showing 6-0 for Wisconsin, adorned the right side of the same page.

After many years of watching the frustrations at Columbus, Fred Gage, a former Wisconsin grid star and longtime broadcaster, and I vowed to erect a plaque commemorating the next Badger victory there on the banks of the Olentangy River, which flows alongside Ohio Stadium. We were too eager to head home, though, and never carried out our plan.

The first of the two "miracles" at Purdue occurred a week before the Ohio State game. Wisconsin trailed, 31-23, with 2:24 remaining in the game. I left the press box and headed for the locker room at that point, content to watch time run out behind the south end zone. Purdue hadn't won in seven games so many Boilermakeı fans decided to leave early and start celebrating.

It took the Badgers just 55 seconds after Purdue's last touchdown to cut their deficit to 31-29. Wright made 79 yards with five straight completions and an interference rap against the Boilermakers. Gerald Green scored from the one but a two-point conversion pass failed.

Purdue needed to take just 79 seconds off the clock to assure the victory. Inexplicably quarterback Scott Campbell ran out of bounds on third down to stop the clock with 25 seconds left. Then Matt Kinzer's punt attempt was fouled by a high snap. He tried to kick with Clint Sims in hot pursuit. The ball skipped low off the ground and Badger linebacker Jim Melka gobbled it up in full stride. He didn't stop until he crossed the goal line. Melka wound up under a huge mass of humanity after his jubilant teammates left the bench area to celebrate.

Melka came to Wisconsin from West Allis Central High School with the reputation of being the best fullback prospect since Alan Ameche but had been switched to linebacker by McClain. "Maybe it's an inborn instinct," he said. "I just saw that goal line and ran for it."

Possibly another linebacker might not have reacted with such dispatch. One Indiana writer, unfamiliar with Melka's prep reputation, asked if he ever ran the ball before. "Yeah, I sure did," replied Melka, who gained 1,600 yards rushing as a senior. "I ran a lot in high school."

Purdue had 21 seconds to retaliate but it wasn't enough. Those fans who left early couldn't believe what they were hearing on their car radios while driving away.

Wisconsin invaded West Lafayette a second straight year for the 10th game in 1983. Again the Boilermakers led with under 3 minutes to play. They scored with 2:35 left to take a 38-35 lead. Wright then hustled the Badgers into their 2-minute offense and led them to Purdue's 13 with 37 seconds left.

Unlike 1982, I learned my lesson and stayed in the press box. I stood close to the elevator and watched the last play, a fourth-and-one from the 13. McClain called timeout to consider his options. Surprisingly Wright passed to tight end Bret Pearson in the end zone while the Boilermakers were looking for Toon. Kevin Rohde's conversion gave Wisconsin a 42-38 victory.

The exciting finish overshadowed an outstanding performance by Toon, who caught eight passes, including several sensational grabs, and gained 252 yards, a Big Ten record at the time. The Boilermakers' reaction smacked of sour grapes. Coach Leon Burtnett said, "They gambled early and it should have cost them the ball game. We had defensive backs go to sleep at times, especially on the 73-yard touchdown."

Toon caught the long one behind Rod Woodson, an Olympic sprinter and an all-American defensive back. Toon's brilliant day enabled Wright to pass for 317 yards on 16 completions in 33 attempts. That figures out to almost 20 yards per completion. Toon averaged 31.5 yards each reception.

Troy King and Wright also complimented each other in Wisconsin's '82 offense. King climaxed his Badger career with four straight 100-yard plus rushing games. He gained 166 against Northwestern, 104 (Indiana), 127 (Iowa) and 132 (Minnesota). After blanking the Gophers, 24-0, Wisconsin received a bid to play in the Independence Bowl Dec. 11.

Rain early in the day at Shreveport, La., slowed the field for the bowl game but Wright didn't seem to mind. He passed to Michael Jones for a 16-yard touchdown. Then he hit Tim Stracka on a slant over the middle and the former Madison West athlete broke away for a touchdown that covered 87 yards, the longest scoring pass in UW history. Rohde kicked both conversions for a 14-3 victory.

Stracka ran about 75 yards after catching the ball and was pulling away from defenders at the end, prompting a series of caustic remarks from Tim's teammates about his speed. He countered, "It depends on who's chasing me. Everybody gives me crap about my speed. I guess I was a little bit faster than everybody who was chasing me. I run a 4.5 (for 40 yards). That's about average speed, but I do OK for myself."

Wright was voted most valuable player after the regular season and dedicated the bowl to his teammates in gratitude for their confidence. "I told some of the players that actions speak louder than words and the only way I can show how grateful I am is to go out and play the best I can and bring a bowl victory back for us."

McClain said defense was the key to the victory. "They were having trouble blocking Krumrie. They tried to single block him a lot, which surprised me because he's too good to be single blocked." Kansas State gained only 65 yards rushing and 192 total yards. Vanden Boom said Krumrie, Darryl Sims and Mark Shumate "just controlled the line of scrimmage."

Wright called the field conditions the worst he ever played on and Stracka agreed. "Yeah, the field was terrible. It was like playing on a sponge, but it was fun. That was oldtime football, playing in the mud and everything. You kind of look forward to games like that once in a while. It was a good time."

Although the Badgers went to a bowl game with a 6-5 record in 1982, they were ignored after a 7-4 mark the following year and stayed home.

Wright ended his college career in Wisconsin's 32-0 victory over Michigan State in '83. He completed 21 of 35 passes for 259 yards against the Spartans, including a 27-yard touchdown throw to Toon.

Toon caught 45 passes, averaging 19.6 yards each reception, and was voted most valuable player that year.

A festive mood prevailed in the Wisconsin locker room after the final game and most Badgers returned to the field for the "fifth quarter." Defensive back Brian Marrow beat a tattoo on a drum, Bob Kobza clanged the cymbals, McClain danced with a cheerleader and Wright tried his lip on a tuba.

Randy left Wisconsin with a degree and UW career records for passing attempts (669), completions (359), yards (4,697) and touchdown passes (34). Wisconsin compiled a 21-14 record during his three years with the varsity. His career was fulfilling.

"If I had stayed at Notre Dame and they had won the national championship, it wouldn't have meant as much as when we won the first bowl game for Wisconsin because we had to work so much harder for it at Wisconsin," he reflected five years after leaving school.

"Coach McClain always had his priorities in the right order and always made you realize what was important and what wasn't important. I'm convinced I'm a better person and have benefited from playing for Dave and the University of Wisconsin in terms of working hard and achieving something a lot of people say you can't achieve."

Wright's career statistics follow:

College STATISTICS

Randy Wright
Quarterback
1981 through 1983

1981

	Att.	Com.	Int.	Yds.	TD	Long
Michigan		Did Not Play				
UCLA	7	4	0	34	0	13
Western Mich.	2	0	0	0	0	0
Purdue		Did Not Play				
Ohio State		Did Not Play				
Michigan State	22	11	0	124	1	36
Illinois		Did Not Play				
Northwestern	3	2	0	19	0	13
Indiana		Did Not Play				
Iowa		Did Not Play				
Minnesota	6	4	1	82	1	49
TOTALS	40	21	1	259	2	49
Tennessee*	21	9	1	123	2	27
Season	61	30	2	382	4	49

1982

	Att.	Com.	Int.	Yds.	TD	Long
Michigan	39	20	1	197	0	21
UCLA	43	21	3	246	2	22
Toledo	22	16	0	184	3	44
Purdue	30	20	0	303	2	54 TD
Ohio State	20	8	1	95	0	17
Michigan State	26	15	1	158	2	24
Illinois	28	13	2	198	1	46 TD
Northwestern	20	12	0	172	1	31 TD
Indiana	17	9	0	149	0	52
Iowa	40	21	5	278	1	52
Minnesota	21	10	0	129	1	28 TD
TOTALS	306	165	13	2109	13	54 TD
Kansas State**	24	9	0	183	2	87 TD
Season	330	174	13	2292	15	87 TD

1983

	Att.	Com.	Int.	Yds.	TD	Long
Northern Illinois	17	9	0	124	0	29
Missouri	19	12	1	114	2	27
Michigan	29	11	2	89	2	32 TD
Northwestern	26	18	1	219	2	22 TD
Illinois	34	15	4	218	1	45
Minnesota	18	11	1	146	1	17
Indiana	19	12	0	199	4	37 TD
Ohio State	39	23	4	319	3	46
Iowa	54	25	1	325	1	44 TD
Purdue	33	16	2	317	2	73 TD
Michigan State	35	21	2	259	1	27 TD
TOTALS	323	173	18	2329	19	73 TD

Career Totals

Att.	Com.	Int.	Yds.	TD	Long
669	359	32	4697	34	73 TD

Including Bowl Games

Att.	Com.	Int.	Yds.	TD	Long
714	377	33	5003	38	87 TD

* Garden State Bowl

** Independence Bowl

Stony Westphal

"I'm sick of this team losing. You know how it is. They've been losing for as long as you and I can remember. I want to win."

— *John Westphal*
Safety

Every football squad needs a "Stony" Westphal, whose personality and competitive fire I once described "as refreshing as a May breeze off Lake Monona."

I also noted in a 1980 column, "In this era of pampered pitchers, fried forwards and spoiled safeties, John Westphal brings the entire athletic world crashing down into a field of reality, or at least to what the whole thing should be all about."

Westphal was a 21-year-old junior defensive safety when I first noticed him at Camp Randall, executing every assignment, whether with the scout team or covering kickoffs, playing as if a trip to the Rose Bowl hung in the balance at every workout.

"It's a lot of fun," Westphal said then. "I wanted to play for this team all my life. It doesn't take any psyching up for me."

The 5-foot-11 190-pound Janesville native possessed just fair speed because of three knee operations. He ran as hard as Harland Carl or Al Toon. It just took him a little longer to arrive at his destination.

"I'm kind of different from most guys," he explained. "I'm a Janesville boy and I used to come up to all the games when I was a little kid. A-Train Thompson and Grape Juice (Johnson) and Rufus (Ferguson) were my heroes. I used to be one of those little kids down at the end of the tunnel getting chin straps.

"I'm up here now and I want to play. I've wanted to play here my whole life, any chance I can get. My whole goal is to play here and win. I'm sick of this team losing. You know how it is. They've been losing for as long as you and I can remember. I want to win."

Westphal came from a distinguished Badger background. His father, the late Fred Westphal, graduated from the university in 1959 and is considered one of the best, if not the best swimmer ever to compete for the UW.

John lettered in football, track and swimming at Janesville Craig High School. He tried wrestling, too, but gave it up because of his knee.

"I had three knee operations and couldn't wrestle anymore so I started to swim, but it was more to just keep in shape for football and track. I don't have a knee here. That's why I run only 4.7."

He was captain and most valuable player of Craig's 1977 football team and a captain of the South team in the Shrine All-Star game the next summer.

John was a throwback to the days of 60-minute players who wore leather helmets without face masks, canvas pants and shoes with square cleats. They never left a game unless carried off the field.

He agreed. "That's what I'm trying to say. I'm from another era, I think. I don't have any respect for my uniform, cleanliness or anybody's body, including my own. I play on emotion mostly.

"You know how it is now? Here's my feeling. Here's the way it is now with my teammates. It's computer football. It's numbers. You've got guys 6-4, 250 and they run a 4.6. They bring 'em in here and make 'em into a guy with a lot of desire and stuff. I'm 20 years behind the times. I'm one of those little guys who wants to play but doesn't have all the numbers. You know?"

John was popular with his teammates. They called him "Stony" for reasons I couldn't fathom until he told me. He explained.

"With a name like John, I like that (Stony). That's a long story and I didn't even understand it till this year. Larry Spurlin, when we were freshmen out at the seminary, gave me that name.

"Okay, try to get this straight. Some guy in Georgia is a barber. He used to take black guys into his barber shop, put a bowl on their head and cut around it so they'd look like Chinamen and could work on the railroad and make drinking money. Okay? I came in and I supposedly had a bowl haircut, so he called me Stony 'cause the barber's name was Stony. That's what they call me. That's all right. You know?"

John was a walk-on, which means he had no football scholarship, although he might have gotten some aid his senior year. Although noticing him at workouts, I couldn't find him at the training table in Camp Randall after practice. While all his scholarship teammates headed for sumptuous catered chow in the "W" Club Annex, Westphal would jump on his bike and head for his apartment to fix himself some macaroni and cheese or whatever.

I found so much inequity in that. He practiced as hard, and probably a lot harder than anybody on the squad. But rules are rules and only so many players were allowed at the training table. John shrugged it off.

He made his first trip with the Badgers to Ohio State in 1979 and experienced that horrendous 59-0 debacle. He also went west in '80 when the Badgers lost unceremoniously to UCLA, 35-0. Those humiliations seared his Badger soul. But he did see California.

"Yeah, I've never been anywhere," he laughed. "I went to Disneyland and everything. But the loss wrecked the whole thing. I went out there to win. I haven't done a lot of what I've wanted to do here, but it's a start. They see I want to play. Then I start moving up. Guys get hurt. Then I can fill in if they get confidence in me."

The '80 team finished a disappointing 4-7 but in 1981, Westphal's senior year, the Badgers compiled a 7-4 record and played in the Garden State Bowl after becoming the first Wisconsin team ever to beat Michigan, Purdue and Ohio State in the same season. He was the sparkplug of Badger special teams and an integral part of Wisconsin's first bowl team in 19 years. His enthusiasm was infectious whether in practice or big games.

I remember talking with him after his last practice, two nights before the '81 Minnesota game, and he admitted, "I'm kind of sad, obviously. I've been playing football for a long time and won't be playing it again. But, then again, it's kind of nice to be ending on a positive note. We've been playing well, so that's a nice way to end it. I'd say I'm satisfied.

"I'm still kind of disappointed we didn't come through when we had to. I wasn't prepared for not going to the Rose Bowl. I always thought all along we were going and when we finally found out we're not, I was disappointed in that.

"But other than that, beating those teams (Michigan, Purdue and Ohio State) was great. I was there (at Ohio State) when we got beat, 59-to-zip. That was the worst feeling in my life. Beating those guys and finally doing it to somebody like we did to Northwestern, that was real exciting.

"But I'd do it over because I came here trying to see if I could make it. I probably could have gone to a small college in the state, made it and played. I came here and found out maybe I couldn't make it on defense. But I can contribute and I think I did contribute a little. So, I'd do it over."

John Westphal left the University of Wisconsin a proud "W" man, having won letters in 1980 and '81. He played football games on both coasts and made a host of friends.

Back in 1980 I wrote, "Years from now, when I'm retired and recalling guys who wore No. 7, I'll remember Mickey Mantle, Bob Waterfield, Hank Luisetti and John Westphal."

The pampered pitchers, fried forwards and spoiled safeties are still around. I am retired now and still remember "Ol' No. 7" going full bore on kickoffs. John Westphal is what college football is all about, or should be, especially on the shores of Lake Mendota.

Al Toon

"Al is one of those receivers you can throw high and outside to and have all the confidence he's going to catch it."

— *Randy Wright*
Quarterback

Randy Wright once said you can't describe Al Toon's talent, you have to watch him.

Toon, who owns all Wisconsin career records for pass receiving, put an exclamation mark on Wright's assessment at Purdue in 1983 when he caught eight passes for 252 yards and set a Big Ten record. More important than the record was the fact that Toon's performance played such a key role in the 42-38 victory. Besides catching a touchdown pass, Toon made an acrobatic grab near the sidelines for a 27-yard gain on the winning drive. Purdue fans couldn't believe what they saw and even Wisconsin partisans, used to such receptions, watched in amazement.

Dave McClain called that catch "unreal" and Purdue coach Leon Burtnett just shrugged and said "unbelievable."

Rod Woodson, the Boilermaker defensive back Toon beat on his 73-yard touchdown, said, "He's a good receiver but he got a couple of what I call lucky touchdowns." What's unusual about that statement was the fact that Toon scored only the one touchdown. Al was making so many brilliant catches all over the field, everything he did was magnified.

That performance at Purdue ranks with Ron VanderKelen's 33 completions in 48 passes in the Rose Bowl and Billy Marek's 304 yards rushing against Minnesota as far as Wisconsin football is concerned. It might even be more remarkable because Al set a Big Ten record for yards gained.

Including the 1984 Hall of Fame game, Toon's career numbers show

131 receptions for 2,103 yards and 19 touchdowns. His season highs were 54 receptions in 1984 and 881 yards, an average gain of 19.9 yards, and nine touchdowns in '83.

When Al came out of Newport News, Va., Menchville High School he was more highly touted as a trackman than a football player. He was short on gridiron experience but keen football observers, especially Wisconsin coaches, could see he had an untapped wealth of raw talent. He showed signs of that brilliance finishing second to Tim Stracka in receiving with 32 catches for 472 yards and five touchdowns in 1982.

Al blossomed in '83 and became one of the premier receivers in the country. He caught 45 passes, including 18 in the last two games. His 252 yards at Purdue not only set a Big Ten record but was the single game high in NCAA Division I that year.

His 45 receptions produced 881 yards, which broke the school record of 817 set by Pat Richter in 1961. His nine touchdown catches also broke Richter's mark of eight established 22 years earlier.

He caught 38 passes in Big Ten games as a junior and that equaled a record set by Tom McCauley in 1966. Seven of his touchdowns were scored in conference games and that, too, equaled Richter's '61 record. The 788 yards gained on those 38 receptions eclipsed the mark of 656 set by Richter, also in '61.

When the season ended, Al's teammates voted him most valuable player. He made all-Big Ten first team and was named Midwest player of the week following his great performance at Purdue.

Toon, who played with a vengeance on the field, was as soft-spoken and unpretentious as Billy Marek once the competition stopped. "My performance came on a lot better than I expected," he said. "I didn't expect to receive as many honors as I got. I thought I had some possibilities of making all-Big Ten but not getting (Midwest) player of the week and breaking all these records. I'm really happy with my performance."

He was especially pleased with the most valuable player award, saying, "It means a lot to me. If the team acknowledges me, I know the team cares for me. I'm honored."

McClain was credited with the understatement of the year after the Purdue game: "He was banged up coming into the game and did a gutsy job. I'll tell you one thing, he's a fairly good receiver."

Wright knew on what side his bread was buttered. "Al is one of those receivers you can throw high and outside to and have confidence he's going to catch it. We design plays for him to make spectacular catches."

Toon went into his senior season with a new quarterback, Mike Howard. Always a student of football and continually striving for excellence, Al worked harder than anybody in preseason that August. "Right now I'm continuing to learn more about the entire offense, not just my position," he said. "That helps a lot. It lets you know ahead of time what's going to happen."

Nobody appreciated Toon more than Fred Jackson, McClain's receiver coach then. He discounted all the pressure under which Al entered the '84 season. "He's the kind of guy who can handle it," Jackson said. "I'm glad it's happening to him because a lot of times you look at some guys and they can't handle the pressure because of the size of their heads. He's not a guy who's like that. He believes in himself but he believes he can always do something to improve himself. There's not going to be a situation where he's going out of here big-headed about things."

Al enjoyed another outstanding year in '84, catching 50 passes during the regular season and four more in the Hall of Fame Bowl. His yardage fell below 1983 and he caught only five scoring passes compared with nine the year before. But the Badgers compiled a 7-3-1 record, the best in McClain's eight years.

Al made all-Big Ten again and was voted UW most valuable player for the second straight year, prompting this response, "It's an honor. I'm just glad I had the opportunity to make it twice. It makes you feel good knowing that you're respected by your teammates."

Toon added a new dimension as a senior. He became an excellent blocker and this ability excited pro scouts.

"Al is one of the best blockers I have seen at his position," McClain praised. And, Al credited that improvement in his game for being voted MVP again.

Although Toon never concentrated on his track career, he still won Big Ten triple jump championships indoors and outdoors. He set a UW indoor record with a 53-7¾ triple jump and sailed 54-7½ outdoors. He also competed in the hurdles and long jump.

Toon went on to an outstanding National Football League career with the New York Jets. He finished consistently among the leading pass receivers and led the NFL in 1988 with 93 catches.

He never led the Big Ten in receiving and Badger fans often complained Wisconsin quarterbacks didn't throw to him enough. Long after his UW career ended Al discounted those insinuations that he should have caught more passes. He explained quarterbacks looked for him first on practically every pass play but he was always being double-covered. Consequently Wright and Howard usually had to look for a secondary receiver. Al said he caught so many more passes with the Jets because opposing defensive backs couldn't double-team him in the NFL. Many of his teammates were equally adept at catching the football so he was open more.

Wisconsin fans later delighted at the sound of "Toon! Toon! Toon!" emanating from the Meadowlands when they watched the Jets on television. They remembered where that chant originated when SRO crowds jammed historic Camp Randall in the early 1980s.

Toon's career statistics follow:

College**STATISTICS**

Al Toon

Wide Receiver
1982 through 1984

1982

	No.	Yds.	TD	Long
Michigan	2	17	0	10
UCLA	2	30	0	16
Toledo	4	53	2	19 TD
Purdue	3	31	0	16
Ohio State	4	50	0	17
Michigan State	5	71	1	24
Illinois	2	88	1	46 TD
Northwestern	3	34	0	18
Indiana	3	40	0	16
Iowa	3	36	1	21 TD
Minnesota	1	22	0	22
Kansas State*	Injured - Did Not Play			
TOTALS	32	472	5	46 TD

1983

	No.	Yds.	TD	Long
Northern Illinois	2	17	0	9
Missouri	5	76	2	27
Michigan	0	0	0	0
Northwestern	7	94	1	18
Illinois	2	54	1	35 TD
Minnesota	1	17	0	17
Indiana	1	37	1	37 TD
Ohio State	3	49	1	22 TD
Iowa	6	136	1	44 TD
Purdue	8	252	1	73 TD
Michigan State	10	149	1	27 TD
TOTALS	45	881	9	73 TD

1984

	No.	Yds.	TD	Long
Northern Illinois	4	80	1	27 TD
Missouri	9	117	2	24 TD
Michigan	4	53	0	16
Northwestern	0	0	0	0
Illinois	8	112	0	31
Minnesota	6	95	0	43
Indiana	1	8	0	8
Ohio State	5	55	0	21
Iowa	3	36	0	15
Purdue	7	118	2	41 TD
Michigan State	3	28	0	12
Kentucky**	4	48	0	21
TOTALS	54	750	5	43

Career Totals

No.	Yds.	TD	Long
127	2055	19	73 TD

Including Bowl Games

No.	Yds.	TD	Long
131	2103	19	73 TD

* Independence Bowl

** Hall of Fame Bowl

The Linemen

"It has been said that if you are hiding from the law, you should join a football team and play in the offensive or defensive line."

— Mike Chapman
Cedar Rapids Gazette

I committed an embarrassing gaffe in 1982 when I wrote a feature on the 30th anniversary of Wisconsin's 1952 Big Ten co-championship football success. That team gave the university its first grid title in 40 years.

I expounded on the running of Alan Ameche and Harland Carl, the passing of Jim Haluska and great defensive exploits of Don Voss, John Dixon, Mark Hoegh and Burt Hable, but nothing about the offensive linemen.

That was unpardonable neglect and I apologized in a later column to such stalwarts as George Steinmetz, Clarence Stensby, Dave Suminski, George Simkowski, Don Ursin, Charlie Berndt, Art Prchlik and the rest. As I wrote then, "I heard quite a bit of criticism for my oversight, mostly from Steinmetz, Stensby, Suminski, Simkowski, Ursin, Berndt and Prchlik."

I added, "I jest. Those unselfish journeymen in shoulder pads were so used to trudging through the trenches in anonymity, another rebuff from some latter-day journalist was hardly noticed by them. Yes, and the moon is made of green cheese."

Steinmetz, a prominent Madison surgeon, did chide me goodnaturedly about my oversight. I admitted I was not the first to overlook offensive linemen and wouldn't be the last.

Ironically, not long after that anniversary story I was in Iowa City covering Wisconsin football and the game program included an article by Mike Chapman of the Cedar Rapids Gazette entitled "Hide Me in the Offensive Line." It included the following, "It's been said that if you are hiding from the law, you should join a football team and play in the offensive or defensive line." Nuff said?

Ameche gained all those yards rushing and never once did I see an asterisk after his records and a notation crediting Steinmetz and Stensby for clearing a continuous path for "The Horse." But who ever said life is fair?

Not many people can reel off the names of the offensive line that blocked so well when Billy Marek rolled up 740 yards in the last three games of the 1974 season. But I'm sure Marek remembers Bob Johnson, Rick Koeck, Joe Norwick, Terry Stieve and John Reimer. All-American tackle Dennis Lick was injured during that streak but he played a major role in Marek's success over the years, too.

I discovered long ago that offensive linemen aren't really offensive at all. Most of them are real nice guys. Defensive linemen are offensive. They have to be. They charge through and attack offensive people. They're actually the wild guys. Most of the time while the offense is on the field, defensive linemen pace the sidelines like caged lions.

Layne McDowell, a former Iowa and pro offensive lineman, once said that psychological studies show that linemen are "the type of people who stick together, go to family picnics and the like."

I noticed that they do have more camaraderie than most athletes. That's because only their parents and a few close friends know who they are. They seldom see their pictures in the paper.

Successful running backs, though, appreciate offensive linemen. Usually after a big game they credit their line. Some take their blockers out to dinner after a big game or when the season ends.

When Troy King strung together four consecutive 100-yard plus rushing games to climax his career, he went out of his way to say nice things about Bob Winckler, Ron Versnik, Mark Subach, Pete Severson and Jeff Dellenbach, who did most of the blocking and made his swan song so memorable.

One reason for the success of Ivan Williamson' s first season at Wisconsin in 1949 was the emergence of Bob Teague as a running back operating behind one of the university's most efficient lines that included Red Wilson, Joe Kelly, Don Knauff, Hal Otterback, Ken Huxhold and Bill Gable.

Gable, recruited by Harry Stuhldreher, was an outstanding guard. He came from Stuhldreher's hometown of Massilon, Ohio, where football borders on a religious experience. Youngsters there learn the game from the minute they start to walk.

Gable was the principal of one of the more amusing stories concerning a Wisconsin football player. He had a strong year in '49 and was highly touted going into the '50 season. The problem was he injured a knee in preseason and never played a minute, yet one magazine named him to its all-American team at the end of the season.

While in Pasadena for the 1963 Rose Bowl, I encountered Gable at one of the Wisconsin practice sessions. We reminisced about his days as a Badger and had a good laugh about him making that all-American team. He probably still hears a lot about that.

Many Wisconsin fans who followed the Badgers back in the 1930s remember the 10-0 victory over Michigan at Ann Arbor when Lynn Jordan returned the opening kickoff 99 yards for a touchdown. Only Jordan and his teammates appreciated the fact that guard Ed Christiansen threw a crunching block clearing the way. Christiansen also hit Illinois passer Les Lindberg the next week, popping the football up in the air and enabling center Al Mahnke to catch it and run 25 yards for the touchdown that beat the Illini, 7-3, in that 1934 game.

Among outstanding linemen in the '30s were Greg Kabat, Mario Pacetti, Frank "Moon" Molinaro, Dave Tobias, John Golemgeske, Ray Davis, Lynn Hovland, Jack Murray, Gene Brodhagen and John "Blackie" O'-Brien.

The '42 team boasted such excellent interior linemen as Bob Baumann, Evan Vogds, Fred Negus, Ken Currier, Lloyd Wasserbach, Paul Hirsbrunner, Dick Thornally and John Roberts. The '59 Big Ten champions featured all-American Dan Lanphear, Jerry Stalcup, Lowell "Gooch" Jenkins, Gerald Kulcinski, Ron Perkins, Bob Nelson, John Gotta, Pete Zouvas and Jim Heineke.

Clearing the way for Lou Holland, Ralph Kurek, Gary Kroner and Ron VanderKelen on the '62 champions were Lee Bernet, Ken Bowman, Ron Henrici, Roger Jacobazzi, Roger Pillath, Jim Schenk, Steve Underwood, Ernie Von Heimburg, John Hohman, Dion Kempthorne, Steve Young, Pete Bruhn and Jim McMillan.

If a Wisconsin coach from any era set out to build a line from scratch, he'd bask in grunt heaven upon finding a Mike Webster on his roster for offense and Tim Krumrie on defense. Webster from Rhinelander and Krumrie from Mondovi are prime reasons why Badger coaches scour the state each year searching for two more like them. Neither one came to the campus as Parade all-Americans or carrying glittering reviews from the so-called experts who rate recruits.

I met Webster for the first time in the office of assistant coach Chuck McBride in 1970. Mike was a freshman who wanted to play defensive tackle. Coaches thought otherwise and made him a center. I'm sure they must have known something because Mike owns four Super Bowl rings today after becoming a Pittsburgh Steelers center against whom all others at his position are measured today.

Webster was John Jardine's first recruit after the latter succeeded John Coatta as head coach in 1969. Jardine once told me about the recruitment of Webster. Mike came to Madison with his father and had lunch with Jardine at the old Loraine Hotel. Jardine offered Mike a scholarship and told him he'd really like to see him playing for Wisconsin. Jardine said Mike stood up, reached over, shook John's hand and said, "I'll be there." He didn't haggle, say he planned more visits or wanted to think it over. It was a deal as far as Mike was concerned.

People say, yeah, it's easy to make a big deal now about Webster because of his pro career. Not so. Those of us who watched Webster for three years at Wisconsin considered him all-American caliber then.

Webster was all-Big Ten and Badger most valuable player in 1973. Wisconsin's first two 1,000-yard rushers, Rufus Ferguson and Billy Marek, both ran behind lines anchored by Webster. Every play starts with the snap of the ball. That triggers the offensive charge. Webster was the key and many of us insisted only the lack of a winning record then prevented Mike from making all-American.

Here's what Webster's thumbnail sketch in the Badger football brochure his senior year noted: "Is an excellent blocker and a rugged competitor . . . Coach Jardine calls him a bona-fide all-American candidate . . . Is an outstanding team leader with a great will to win . . . Works out almost every day and spends at least three days a week in the weight room."

That sounds so similar to what people said and wrote about Webster throughout his career with both the Steelers and the Kansas City Chiefs. He was billed as the strongest man in the NFL in his prime because he outlifted everybody else in competition.

Krumrie, like Webster, was a tireless performer. He started the first game as a freshman and all 46 Wisconsin played during his four-year career. That's almost an unthinkable statistic in an era of overstuffed egos and overcrowded training rooms.

Wisconsin's success during the Dave McClain era helped Krumrie make all-American in 1981 and, of course, he was a big reason for the winning records. He opened '81 with a great game as the Badgers upset No. 1 ranked Michigan. Krumrie was credited with 13 tackles and the Associated Press named him national player of the week. He also made 19 tackles against UCLA, including 15 solos. Tim led the Badgers in tackles in 1980 and '81 and wound up his career as the school's all-time leader in solo stops with 255.

Webster and Krumrie had many things in common, including the fact that each found it difficult to go at anything but top speed. Sometimes coaches want dummy scrimmages run at half or three-quarter speed. These two had trouble with that.

Krumrie always had an open wound on the bridge of his nose. Coaches blamed it on the helmet. Blood usually trickled down his nose from that continuous battering, even after Friday practices, which were light workouts without pads.

I remember Webster running out on the field for one of those "light" Friday workouts while adjusting his forearm pads. Someone on the sidelines hollered, "Hey, Mike, why are you wearing those today?" He looked over with a mischievous scowl and shouted back, "Come on out here and you'll see."

Webster and Krumrie epitomized the best in Wisconsin line play.

All-Time Team

"Face it, all-time teams are designed to create controversy."

— *Tom Butler*
Author

When college football celebrated its centennial in 1969, each Big Ten school was asked to name its all-time team. Wisconsin fans selected 11 familiar names headed by fullback Alan "The Horse" Ameche, a two-time all-American and the Heisman Trophy winner in 1954.

Ameche, the fans' choice as Wisconsin's all-time greatest football player, was picked in a backfield that included Pat Harder, Elroy "Crazylegs" Hirsch and Ron VanderKelen, quarterback of the 1962 Big Ten champions.

Linemen honored were ends Dave Schreiner and Pat Richter along with Robert "Red" Wilson, Howard "Cub" Buck, Arlie Mucks Sr., Dan Lanphear and Ken Bowman. All-Americans in that group besides Ameche were Harder ('42), Schreiner ('41, '42), Richter ('61, '62), Buck ('15), Mucks ('14) and Lanphear ('59).

Hirsch, rushing and interception leader of the great '42 team, later was named the No. 1 flanker for the National Football League's first 50 years following his outstanding career as a pass receiver with the Los Angeles Rams.

Wilson is the only Badger ever to be voted Wisconsin's most valuable player three straight years ('47, '48, '49) and Bowman, center of the '62 champions and co-captain the next year, later played on three Green Bay Packers championship teams, two of them Super Bowl winners.

VanderKelen, Big Ten passing and total offense leader and conference most valuable player in '62, also was co-most valuable player of the '63 Rose Bowl and MVP of the College All-Star game the following August when the collegians upset the Packers, 20-17.

The intervening years produced some new Badger heroes and changes among fan favorites. The Wisconsin State Journal sponsored another election in 1985 to determine how much thinking actually changed. The balloting probably reflected a younger group of voters were participating.

This time Richter and Al Toon were chosen as the offensive ends with Schreiner and Stu Voigt the next two vote-getters. Dennis Lick finished head and shoulders above other tackles. Then came Jeff Dellenbach, Lanphear and Ray Snell.

Terry Stieve, one of Billy Marek's blockers, received most votes among guards, and was followed in order by Charles "Buckets" Goldenberg, Jerry Stalcup, Greg Kabat and Ken Huxhold.

Nobody came close to Mike Webster at center, an all-Big Ten choice in '73. His popularity obviously grew after becoming all-pro with the Pittsburgh Steelers and owner of four Super Bowl rings.

Wilson and Bowman finished in a virtual tie for second place, followed by Gary Messner, Badger captain and all-conference in '54. Fans apparently weren't sure just where Wilson belonged. He also received enough votes at end, a position he played as a senior, to finish fifth among flankers.

Like the original '69 balloting, Ameche received more votes than anybody. He headed the first team backfield with Marek, Hirsch and VanderKelen. The second group of running backs featured Rufus Ferguson, Harder and Harland Carl, a breakaway runner with the '52 Big Ten co-champions. Carl would have been an ideal flanker in modern football because of his pass-catching ability.

VanderKelen won by almost 3-to-1 over runnerup Randy Wright in the quarterback voting. Next came Dale Hackbart, versatile leader of the '59 champions, and John Coatta, record-setting passer in '50 and '51.

Jim Bakken, a quarterback and defensive back in '59, '60 and '61, was the runaway winner as punter. He also edged legendary Pat O'Dea as a kicker. Ken Simmons finished a distant second in punting, an area where Bakken led the Big Ten in '60 and '61. Richter, Mickey McGuire and Hackbart also got votes as punters.

Vince Lamia finished third behind O'Dea as a kicker. If the voting had occurred after '85, it's a given Todd Gregoire would have pressed the leaders. He set the school kick-scoring record of 278 points during his career from '84-'87.

Nose guard Tim Krumrie was the overwhelming leader among defensive players chosen. He received only one vote less than Ameche overall. Other down linemen included Pat O'Donahue, Darryl Sims, Don Voss, Bill

Gregory, Tubby Keeler, Tom Domres, Jim DeLisle, Jim Temp, Bob Kennedy and Buck.

Ken Criter got most votes among linebackers and was followed by Hal Faverty, Dave Ahrens, Jim Melka, Deral Teteak, Dave Crossen, Jim Purnell, Gary Buss and Kyle Borland.

David Greenwood, Richard Johnson and Matt Vanden Boom, whose exploits were still vivid in the minds of voters in '85, received most votes among defensive backs. Johnson and Vanden Boom were first-team all-Americans and Greenwood made the second team. Also getting strong support were Ed Withers, Lawrence Johnson, Hackbart, Steve Wagner, Jim Nettles, Bob Zeman and Hirsch.

Selecting a team like this borders on the impossible. If you ask 20 people for their favorites, chances are no two teams would be exactly the same. Just selecting one era over another causes a major problem. So many younger fans have little information on the so-called oldtimers.

Undoubtedly, when you think of ends today, Richter and Toon stand out. They were Wisconsin's best pass-catchers statistically. However, it's difficult to imagine any all-time Badger team without Schreiner. And, I'm convinced my recollection of him has not become embellished by time.

Schreiner played in an era of single platoon football and was named all-American his junior and senior years. He caught five touchdown passes in 1942 when offenses revolved around the running game. He led the conference in receiving with only 12 catches and four touchdowns in 1941. Dave had great hands and, although he would have made it offensively today, his defense was even better. He probably would play outside linebacker in the era of two-platoon football.

Wisconsin's record book lists 32 touchdown passes of 55 yards or more and Schreiner caught three, more than any other receiver. He combined with John Tennant for 72 yards against Minnesota in '40, with Jack Wink for 71 yards against Marquette in '42, and with Tom Farris for 55 yards against Indiana in '41. He missed another of 70 yards against Minnesota in '42, catching a pass from Hirsch and going all the way. However, officials said he stepped on the out-of-bound line at the Gopher 41 and the play went for a 29-yard gain.

Guys like Red Wilson and Hackbart suffered in voting because of their versatility. Wilson was MVP two years as a center and once as an end, who could catch the football, block like a tight end and play outside linebacker. He got votes at both positions. Hackbart finished third among quarterbacks, sixth among defensive backs, fifth among punters and received some votes as a running back.

Coatta, who wound up fourth among quarterbacks, said of Hackbart, "He took a team to the Rose Bowl that shouldn't even have been within sniffing distance. He played both ways. You talk about leadership and all-around abilities!" Put Hackbart or Coatta in the same backfield with second team running backs Harder, Ferguson, Harland Carl or Jug Girard and that team would win a lot of games.

Carl, when healthy, was as explosive as any runner who ever carried a football. Girard passed, ran, punted, kicked field goals and wound up as a wide receiver with the Detroit Lions.

Mickey McGuire, a hero of the early '30s, was a favorite of Bill Nathenson, a Chicago lawyer, Madison native and longtime Badger booster. Nathenson considered McGuire Wisconsin's all-time most valuable player. He recalled when McGuire beat Minnesota almost single-handedly in '32 by scoring all three Badger touchdowns, including an 88-yard return of the opening kickoff. Earlier that year, playing defensive back, Mickey came from 15 yards behind a Marquette ballcarrier to make a touchdown-saving tackle and preserve a 7-2 victory.

The previous year, coach Glen Thistlethwaite moved McGuire from halfback to quarterback for one game against Purdue and he led the Badgers to a 21-14 upset victory. McGuire possessed the dramatic flair of Hirsch and the charisma of Ferguson.

Here's the breakdown of how many athletes received votes at each position — 18 ends, 23 tackles, 26 guards, 10 centers, 11 quarterbacks, 25 running backs, eight kickers, 14 punters, 39 down linemen, 21 linebackers and 21 defensive backs.

Center is an illustrious position in Wisconsin history. Only fullbacks produced more outstanding players than the center position. The cream of the crop included Webster, Wilson, Bowman, Negus and Messner.

Negus holds a unique distinction among Wisconsin football players. An Ohio product himself, he probably is the only Badger ever to play on winning teams all three times he faced Ohio State. Those included Wisconsin victories in '42, 17-7, and '46, 20-7, and Michigan's 45-7 trouncing of the Buckeyes in '43, when he was a Marine trainee at Ann Arbor. Negus made the all-Big Ten team as a sophomore in '42 and was voted Wisconsin's most valuable player after the '46 season.

These centers all did well after leaving school. Webster, of course, became the premier center of the National Football League. Negus and Messner headed their own companies, Wilson became a bank president after playing baseball for 10 years in the major leagues, and Bowman an attorney.

I think this has to do with being a center. When you think of bending over, passing a football between your legs and then trying to block an opponent coming off a two or three-point stance, the prospect is scary. There isn't a more awkward position in sports. That's why I believe centers become sucessful after football. Most are convinced there's more to life and plan for the day they can straighten up and fly right.

Two other Badgers who would seem to deserve more recognition than they get from fans are Don Kindt and Carl Silvestri, a pair of halfbacks from the '40s and '60s, respectively. Kindt was a triple threat back in '43 and then went off to fight in Europe during World War II, finishing his college career in '45 and '46. He shared the Big Ten scoring lead in '45. Later he played nine years for the Chiago Bears and was one of their last two-way performers.

I always figured if you had all the great Badgers on a football field and were choosing up sides, Hackbart and Kindt might be the first guys chosen. Kindt could have excelled at guard, tight end, linebacker or fullback as well as halfback.

Silvestri also was such a versatile athlete that Milt Bruhn needed him on defense in '63 and '64, although he was an outstanding running back, too. He averaged 6.2 yards a carry in '62 and caught three passes for 51 yards in the Rose Bowl. Despite concentrating on defense, he carried the ball 156 times in college for 807 yards, a 5.2 average.

The quarterback voting wasn't surprising except it seemed odd Jim Miller didn't receive a single vote in the polling. Following the first four, others receiving votes were Jim Haluska, Neil Graff, Bob Petruska, Ron Miller, Gregg Bohlig, Jack Wink and Ed J. "Toad" Crofoot.

Haluska played a key role in the '52 co-championship. Wink quarterbacked the great '42 team but was overshadowed by some legends. Ron Miller led the Big Ten in passing in '60 and '61.

Jim Miller did a more than adequate job when he assumed the quarterback spot in '53 after Haluska broke his leg playing baseball that summer. Jim ran for six touchdowns and threw for six more and was the Big Ten passing leader. Wisconsin finished third behind co-champions Michigan State and Illinois (5-1), but few people remember a 20-19 loss to Ohio State cost the Badgers (4-1-1) an undisputed title that season.

The next year Wisconsin shared second place with a 5-2 record and was 7-2 overall. Miller finished second to Ameche in team rushing, while leading the Badgers in passing, pass interceptions and punt returns. Playing safety he intercepted six passes and returned them 117 yards. He returned 18 punts 141 yards, a 7.8 average. He also returned three kickoffs 70 yards, a 23.3 average, best on the team. Jim Miller could play football.

Face it, all-time teams are designed to create controversy.

The Last Hurrah

"What can you say? It was a great effort by an excellent bunch of guys."

— *Dave McClain*
Head Coach

Wisconsin's 1984 team, with Mike Howard at quarterback, compiled a 7-3-1 regular-season record, the best in Dave McClain's tenure as head coach. These Badgers eventually lost to Kentucky, 20-19, in the Hall of Fame Bowl at Birmingham, Ala.

Along the way the Badgers won a stunning victory at Missouri, 35-34, with 28 points in the fourth quarter, and upset eventual Big Ten champion Ohio State, 16-14, in the rain at Camp Randall. They also lost to Michigan, 20-14; Illinois, 22-6; and Minnesota, 17-14; and were tied at Iowa, 10-10. McClain never could beat Iowa or Illinois and was 1-7 against the Wolverines. Those teams cost him some lofty finishes in the Big Ten and bids from more prestigious bowls.

The Badgers outgained Michigan, 385 yards to 316, and tailback Larry Emery accounted for 185 rushing. But Wisconsin also lost five fumbles.

Illinois got one touchdown and five field goals, while the Badgers scored on two Todd Gregoire field goals. It seemed like Australian football.

Two Rickey Foggie touchdown runs and another field goal sank the Badgers against Minnesota. Wisconsin jumped to a 10-0 lead at Iowa, then went into a shell and let the Hawkeyes rally in the second half.

I wrote after the Missouri game that Wisconsin fans sitting in Faurot Field at Columbia were preparing a Requiem for the Badgers, who trailed 28-7 starting the fourth quarter. Suddenly, though, the patient made a miraculous recovery.

The comeback started when Bobby Taylor blocked a Tiger punt on the first play of the fourth quarter and Richard Johnson grabbed the loose football on the Missouri one and stepped into the end zone for a touchdown. Less than 2 minutes later Johnson partially blocked another punt and Wisconsin took possession at Missouri's 37. Mike Howard passed nine yards to Al Toon for another touchdown on the sixth play.

Midway through the period the Badgers drove 66 yards in six plays, climaxed by Howard's 24-yard scoring pass to Toon. Gregoire's conversion tied the score at 28-all. Michael Reid's interception on Missouri's 35 set up the go-ahead touchdown. Howard passed to Toon for 14 yards and Marck Harrison raced 21 yards on a draw play for the score. Missouri fans sat in stunned disbelief.

The Tigers scored a touchdown with 1:28 left but their two-point conversion pass was dropped in the end zone. It marked the second straight loss to Wisconsin because they failed on a two-point attempt.

Ohio State came to Madison for the eighth game on a rainy afternoon. So many Ohio State games seem to have been played in the rain. The Buckeyes were 6-1, having lost only to Purdue, 28-23.

Wisconsin's camp lacked the usual bravado because Emery suffered a severe knee injury at Indiana the previous week, underwent surgery and was lost for the season. He was the Badgers' leading rusher with 675 yards and a 6.2 average.

Ohio State's Keith Byars arrived as one of college football's premier attractions. He led the Big Ten and the nation in per-game averages for rushing (117 yards), scoring (14.6 points) and all-purpose running (239.3 yards). Mike Tomczak was the Buckeye quarterback. Some of my colleagues at the State Journal were laying bets on how many yards Byars would gain against the Badgers. Something like 250 was a conservative estimate.

Marck Harrison, who experienced somewhat of a checkered career up to that point, started at tailback in place of Emery. He had quit the team once, disgruntled because he wasn't playing much. The ironic twist was he grew up in Columbus and had always hoped to play for the Buckeyes but was never offered a scholarship.

Harrison couldn't have dreamed what happened to him that day and such a script would have embarrassed a Hollywood writer. Not only did the Badgers win, 16-14, but Harrison gained 203 yards rushing to Byars' 142. Marck had only 187 yards total after the first seven games.

Wisconsin scored on Howard's 34-yard pass to Thad McFadden and three Gregoire field goals. The Buckeyes had one final chance, starting from their own 20 with 59 seconds left. Three straight Tomczak passes fell incomplete and on fourth down Byars caught a short toss and headed upfield. He found linebacker Craig Raddatz in his path and they collided with the ferocity of two charging rams. Byars fell to the wet turf one yard short of a first down. Wisconsin took possession with 47 seconds left. Howard dropped to his knee twice and it was over.

The Buckeyes, who sidetracked Wisconsin's title chances so many times in the 1950s, still won the Big Ten championship with a 7-2 record. The Badgers tied for fourth at 5-3-1. Harrison, who gained 225 yards in 39 carries against Purdue two weeks later, finished with 848 for the season. Howard passed for 2,127 yards and 11 touchdowns. Toon caught 54 passes for 750 yards, scored five touchdowns and was named most valuable player for the second straight year.

The trip to Birmingham offered some consolation but the one-point loss soured the occasion. Once again the Badgers couldn't stand prosperity, this time a 13-0 lead in the second quarter. They let Kentucky rally and beat them with a 52-yard field goal.

Wisconsin still had a shot at victory when Gregoire set up for a field goal try from the 15 with 2 minutes left. But holder Bob Kobza bobbled the snap. He then threw a lazy pass into the end zone and it was intercepted.

Badger hopes flickered when the Wildcats were forced to punt from their 24 with a minute left. But, Ken Stills roughed the punter and the flame died. Wisconsin left Birmingham nursing a serious case of self-doubt.

The wheels started to come off Wisconsin's red machine in 1985. McClain struggled through his first losing season in five years, a 5-6 record. Toon had been drafted by the New York Jets in the first round that winter and with him gone the Badgers lost much of their pizazz.

McClain experienced one last hurrah at Ohio State that season when the Badgers beat the Buckeyes for the fourth time in five years, by a 12-7 margin. Gregoire kicked field goals of 49 and 19 yards but Ohio State quarterback Jim Karsatos threw a 37-yard touchdown pass to Chris Carter, and Rich Spangler converted for a 7-6 Buckeye halftime lead.

The first of Michael Reid's three fumble recoveries put the Badgers in possession for their clinching touchdown at the Buckeye 22-yard line with 4:38 left in the third quarter. Four plays later freshman fullback Marvin Artley plunged one yard for a touchdown. Howard's two-point conversion pass was batted down by linebacker Chris Spielman. The five-point cushion was all Wisconsin needed as its defense dominated the rest of the way.

Reid recovered two more fumbles to snuff out Buckeye drives in the fourth quarter. Ohio State seemed ready to score with 9:50 left. Fullback Roman Bates headed for a hole in the center at Wisconsin's five but he lost the ball and Reid smothered it at the four.

Then tight end Ed Taggert caught a short pass from Karsatos but coughed up the football when hit by linebackers Charlie Fawley and Raddatz. Reid recovered again.

Scott Cepicky kept the Buckeyes out of good field position when the Badgers couldn't mount a drive on their last three possessions by lofting punts of 39, 51 and 48 yards.

McClain, who called the '82 victory at Columbus his biggest as a coach, was somewhat more subdued this time and shrugged, "What can you say? It was a great effort by an excellent bunch of guys." Maybe beating Ohio State was becoming old hat to him. He made the front page again. A four-column color picture showed him applauding his victorious team on the way to the locker room.

Raddatz expressed the feeling prevalent in the jubilant locker room. "This makes up for a lot but it still hurts to think what this team could do and what I think this team should have done. That's one of the reasons we have to come back strong next week against Michigan State and get that winning season. This team isn't a bunch of losers."

A winning season never materialized. Michigan State and tailback Lorenzo White buried the Badgers in a snowstorm at Camp Randall, 41-7. "It was a horrible performance of a football game," McClain said. "It's amazing that a week ago you could play so emotional and be like we were today and play so poorly."

McClain, a consummate college coach who reveled in his chosen profession, never paced the sidelines again. He collapsed in a sauna room in Camp Randall and died of cardiac arrest Monday, April 28, 1986, two days after spring practice ended. He was only 48. The news shocked everyone who knew and respected him. His death was a tragedy for his wife Judy and their family and the university.

He was the fifth person connected with the Wisconsin football program to die since 1979. Defensive back Jay Seiler suffered a brain injury in spring practice that year and died April 7. Flanker Wayne Souza drowned in Lake Monona July 21, 1979. John Tringali, a reserve defensive tackle, died in his Madison apartment of unknown causes Feb. 1, 1984.

Dick Scesniak, 44, an assistant under McClain during the 1982 season who became head coach at Kent State, died of a heart attack after jogging a month before McClain's death.

Such tragedies shocked the UW program throughout the second half of the century. Ivan Williamson, architect of Wisconsin's most successful modern football resurgence, succumbed Feb. 19, 1969, of "irreversible brain damage" following a fall on a basement staircase at his Maple Bluff home. He had been relieved of his athletic director duties and assigned to the physical education school the previous month. Ironically, he died the same night Elroy Hirsch was being interviewed for the vacated AD job.

Senior end Tim Klosek of Whiting, Ind., died July 4, 1972, in a highway accident on the outskirts of Madison.

John Jardine, a popular coach whose wide open football brought crowds back to Camp Randall in the 1970s, died at the age of 54 on March 23, 1990. He had been the recipient of a heart transplant the previous June. Doctors said the cause was "heart failure, not rejection of the new heart."

Although a Purdue graduate, Jardine remained in Madison after resigning as head coach in 1977. He worked in the insurance business and became a radio and television commentator at Badger football games and one of the UW's most enthusiastic boosters. He helped both Pat Richter and Barry Alvarez while they settled into their new jobs as athletic director and football coach.

"He was so excited and happy to be involved in the football program again," Richter said. Alvarez added, "In the short time that I had been here, he and I had become very close and I considered him a very close friend and somebody who helped me tremendously."

Dan Jardine said the last weeks were among the happiest in his father's life because of that association with Richter and Alvarez.

Another tragedy occurred in 1967 when Badger defensive back Melvin Walker's left leg was amputated below the knee following a collision during the Minnesota game. Attending physicians described the damage to Walker's left knee as "one of the worst on-field limb injuries we have ever seen." When a blood clot developed following surgery at Minneapolis, amputation became necessary.

The NCAA placed Wisconsin on one-year probation twice in the 1980s. Those infractions embarrassed the university and clouded positive aspects of McClain's tenure. The first came in January, 1982, without sanctions because of "irregularities" when recruiting offensive lineman Carlton Walker. The second occurred in November of 1983 and also prohibited the Badgers from appearing on television for a season. This resulted from an alumnus illegally puchasing airline tickets for recruits Ken Stills and Tyler Carbone.

Wisconsin football fell on hard times following McClain's death but the feeling persists that latent Wisconsin "spirit" will explode at the least sign of success. I touched on that Badger psyche in a Wisconsin State Journal column Sept. 14, 1973.

"Nebraska stadium bulges at the seams with 76,000 for a team that is expected to contend for the national championship each year, while some 78,000 clamor to watch the Badgers, hoping they might sneak out a victory and maybe, just possibly, salvage a 6-5 season.

"And those avid believers still hoist their steins, sing 'On, Wisconsin' and sneak in an occasional chorus of 'If You Want to be a Badger' in their favorite bistros afterward, win or lose.

"Those rituals have been repeated by generations of students through a Victorian hiatus, the Noble Experiment, the Great Depression, wars and campus turmoil."

Football coaches traditionally remain incurable optimists. To them success always hunkers just around the corner. Inevitably, then, Wisconsin fans live for each new "turnaround."

One Man's Opinion

"The teams, the players, the games, the performances, plays and personalities that made Badger football what it is today."

— *Tom Butler*
Author

When the University of Wisconsin celebrated 100 years of intercollegiate football in 1988, several interested observers were asked to submit their top 10 Badger teams, players, games, performances and personalities for the Badgesr game program. Following are my selections with a few modifications made since then.

PLAYERS

1. Alan Ameche — A great player at his best in the toughest situations.
2. Elroy Hirsch — Provided the spark that made the '42 team exceptional.
3. Pat Harder — Versatile athlete whose play inspired his teammates.
4. Dave Schreiner — Most talented two-way end ever at Wisconsin.
5. Jug Girard — One of the two or three best triple-threat halfbacks ever at UW.
6. Ron VanderKelen — Did more with his opportunity than any Badger ever.
7. Billy Marek — Possessed that intangible all great football runners have.
8. Pat Richter — Great pass receiver at his best in clutch situations.
9. Red Wilson — Only three-time most valuable player in UW history, twice as a center and once at end.
10. Mike Webster and Dennis Lick — Possessed the best technique of all Badger offensive linemen.

TEAMS

1. 1942 — First UW team to win eight games since 1905; great personnel that provided excitement and pride for the first time in many years.
2. 1951 — The "Hard Rocks" featured the best UW defensive unit plus a fine offense that was overshadowed by defenders.
3. 1962 — Averaged 32.2 points a game and never gave up more than two touchdowns a game until the Rose Bowl.
4. 1952 — Not as good defensively as '51, but the first Badger champion in 40 years.
5. 1912 — Must have been good because the UW hasn't had an unbeaten team since.
6. 1958 — Better than the '59 championship team, losing only to eventual champion Iowa.
7. 1981 — Beat Michigan, Ohio State and Purdue. 'Nuff said!
8. 1974 — Up and down team but exciting with Billy Marek.
9. 1932 — Lost only to Purdue by one point.
10. 1928 — Beat Notre Dame and Michigan, shut out five opponents and lost only to Minnesota by a touchdown.

GAMES

1. 1942 Ohio State — Beat the nation's No. 1 team, 17-7, with all eyes on Madison (too bad there was no television).
2. 1953 Illinois — Trounced the unbeaten Illini, 34-7, with a perfect team performance.
3. 1962 Minnesota — The Badgers needed this 14-9 victory to win the Big Ten.
4. 1962 Northwestern — Wildcats came here No. 1 but the country took notice of VanderKelen and Co. after the 37-6 victory.
5. 1963 Rose Bowl — A 42-37 loss but Wisconsin's comeback got more notoriety than USC's victory.
6. 1982 Ohio State — The 6-0 victory was Wisconsin's first at Columbus since 1918.
7. 1981 Michigan — The Wolverines came to Madison No. 1 in the country and lost, 21-14.
8. 1969 Iowa — Broke a 23-game winless streak, 23-17, and triggered an unbelievable celebration.
9. 1974 Nebraska — A 21-20 victory gave John Jardine a win over a big-time opponent.
10. 1932 Minnesota — A spectacular day for Mickey McGuire in a 20-13 victory over the arch rival.

PERFORMANCES

1. Ron VanderKelen's 33 completions on 48 passes for 401 yards in '63 Rose Bowl.
2. Billy Marek's 740 yards rushing and 13 touchdowns in the last three games of 1974.
3. Elroy Hirsch's 59-yard run from scrimmage and 14-yard touchdown pass to Dave Schreiner that beat Ohio State in 1942.
4. Al Toon's 252 yards on eight pass receptions against Purdue in 1983.
5. Dale Hackbart against Minnesota in 1959 when he ran for a touchdown, had 149 passing yards, 74 rushing yards, two-point conversion pass, one punt for 56 yards and intercepted a Gopher pass.
6. Alan Ameche's 133 yards rushing on 28 carries, including a 54-yard run, in the 1953 Rose Bowl.
7. Lou Holland's four touchdowns and 71 yards on five carries against Illinois in 1962.
8. Mickey McGuire's three touchdowns, including an 88-yard kickoff return, against Minnesota in 1932.
9. Pat Richter's nine receptions for 170 yards against Illinois in 1961 and 11 catches for 163 yards in the '63 Rose Bowl.
10. Jug Girard's 85- and 63-yard punt returns for touchdowns against Iowa in 1947.

PERSONALITIES

1. Rufus Ferguson — Fans' favorite whose exciting play and touchdown "shuffle" brought crowds back to Camp Randall.
2. Elroy Hirsch — Sensational performer and charismatic leader as athletic director who enhanced UW athletics at a difficult time.
3. Mickey McGuire — An outstanding athlete and a great advertisement for the UW.
4. Alan Ameche — Epitomized the old adage, "the bigger the man the better the person."
5. Dale Hackbart — Agile, mobile, hostile and Wisconsin's best-ever inside the 20-yard line.
6. Harland Carl — Had the fans on the edge of their seats every time he touched the football.
7. Milt Bruhn — An outstanding coach who seemed like everybody's favorite uncle.
8. Tim Krumrie — No Badger ever gave more of himself to UW football.
9. Don Kindt — A great story-teller who could play any position on the field.
10. Pat O'Donahue — A defensive grunt who led the '51 "Hard Rocks," a rowdy group who yielded only 601 rushing yards in nine games.

PLAYS

1. John Tennant's touchdown pass to Ray Kreick with time running out and Bob Ray's conversion that beat Purdue, 14-13, in 1940.
2. The "bounce pass" from Randy Wright to Al Toon to Jeff Nault for a touchdown against Illinois in 1982.
3. Jack Wink's 101-yard interception return for a touchdown against Great Lakes in 1942.
4. Jess Cole's touchdown pass to John Williams for 71 yards against Michigan in 1981.
5. Alan Ameche's 29-yard touchdown run in a 6-0 victory over Michigan State in 1954.
6. Gregg Bohlig's touchdown pass to Jeff Mack for 77 yards that beat Nebraska, 21-20, in 1974.
7. Elroy Hirsch's 62-yard touchdown run from scrimmage against Great Lakes in 1942.
8. Jim Melka's scoring run with a blocked punt that beat Purdue in the closing seconds in 1982.
9. Jim Nettles' interception in the end zone, halting Minnesota's last threat in 1962.
10. Bud Seelinger's six-yard touchdown pass to Mark Hoskins in the closing seconds that beat Northwestern, 20-19, in 1942.
11. Harland Carl's 40-yard touchdown run that triggered the 34-7 victory over Illinois in 1953.
12. John Coatta's 35-yard touchdown pass to Billy Hutchinson that beat Indiana, 6-0, in the 1951 "snow bowl."
13. Billy Lowe's 98-yard inteception return for a touchdown against Purdue in 1954.
14. Randy Wright's 13-yard touchdown pass to Bret Pearson that beat Purdue in the closing seconds in 1983.
15. Rufus Ferguson's 65-yard touchdown run from scrimmage to launch the victory over Indiana, 30-12, in 1970.
16. Randy Wright's touchdown pass to Tim Stracka for 87 yards against Kansas State in the 14-3 Independence Bowl victory in 1982.
17. Neil Graff's touchdown pass to Larry Mialik for 52 yards with 4:33 left in the 29-16 victory over Penn State in 1970.
18. Harland Carl's circus catch of Jim Miller's pass that beat Iowa, 10-6, in 1953.
19. Dale Hackbart's 64-yard punt return for a touchdown in a 7-7 tie at Ohio State in 1958.
20. Ira Matthews' 100-yard kickoff return for a touchdown against Iowa in 1976.

INDEX

A

Ahrens, Dave - 138, 169
Ali, Muhammad - 112
Altman, Bob - 67, 70, 74, 76
Alvarez, Barry - 177
Ameche, Alan "The Horse" - 15, 44, 46-48, 51-57, 59,62-64, 73, 74, 76,108, 117, 124, 129, 146, 161, 162, 167,168, 171, 179, 181, 182
Amling, Warren - 33
Anderson, Ashley - 23, 24
Armstrong, Ralph - 46
Artley, Marvin - 175
Athan, Dick - 60

B

Bahlow, Ed - 34
Bakke, Walter - 82
Bakken, Jim - 16, 67, 75, 78, 91, 168
Barnhill, Jim - 75
Barnum, Rollie - 75
Barton, George - 34
Bartz, Shorty - 6
Bass, Mike - 144
Bates, Mickey - 52, 62
Bates, Roman - 175
Baugh, Sammy - 128
Baumann, Bob - 19, 20, 24, 163
Beathard, Pete - 98, 100
Bedsole, Hal - 98
Beise, Sheldon - 55
Belisle, Verlyn - 80
Bell, Bobby - 84, 94, 95
Bellin, Roy - 75
Bender, Jack - 9
Bendrick, Ben - 15, 35, 129
Berndt, Charlie - 161
Bernet, Lee - 98, 100, 163
Bertelli, Angelo - 20
Bierele, Bob - 17
Bierman, Bernie - 12
Blackbourn, Lisle Jr. - 37, 40
Blackbourn, Lisle Sr. - 37, 39
Blaska, Duane - 84, 94
Bohlig, Gregg - 119-122, 171, 182
Boodry, Kevin - 123
Borland, Kyle - 145, 169
Bowman, Ken - 91,93, 100, 130, 163, 167, 168, 170
Boyajian, John - 104, 105
Brandt, Harold - 81, 91, 92
Brodhagen, Gene - 163
Broeder, George - 64
Brown, Bill - 70
Brown, Jim - 53
Brown, Paul - 21
Brown, Willie - 99
Bruce, Earle - 69
Bruhn, Milt - 7, 40, 64, 66, 69-71, 73-75, 82-84, 86, 89, 90-92, 98, 99, 103, 104, 107, 171, 181
Bruhn, Pete - 163
Bucciarelli, Gale - 104
Buck, Howard "Cub" - 2, 5, 167, 169
Buehler, Larry - 55
Burns, Jerry - 82
Burtnett, Leon - 147, 155
Burton, Ron - 70
Buss, Gary - 110, 169
Butler, Nate - 110
Butler, Robert "Butts" - 5
Byars, Keith - 174

C

Cairns, Jim - 94
Calhoun, Gene - 75
Calligaro, Len - 23, 129
Campbell, Hugh - 101
Campbell, Joe - 33
Campbell, Scott - 146
Canada, Larry - 119, 123, 133
Carbone, Tyler - 177
Carl, Harland - 32, 44, 46, 48, 59-64, 73, 74, 76, 77, 151, 161, 168, 170, 181, 182
Carlson, Ron - 100

Caroline, J.C. - 52, 62
Carter, Cris - 175
Cassady, Howard "Hopalong" - 63
Casserly, Hank - 5
Cassiano, Dick - 11
Cepickey, Scott - 176
Chapman, Mike - 161, 162
Chappuis, Bob - 35
Charles, David - 182
Chickerneo, John - 11
Christensen, Gwynn - 35, 40
Christiansen, Ed - 163
Christman, Paul - 16
Cisco, Jeff - 140
Coatta, John - 44, 46-48, 64, 104, 106, 107, 109, 110, 112, 164, 168-170, 182
Cochems, Eddie - 2, 5
Cohee, Kevin - 123
Cole, Jess - 137-144, 182
Coughlin, Roundy - 10, 15, 17, 96
Cregan, Bill - 75
Crisler, Fritz - 35
Criter, Ken - 169
Crofoot, Ed J. "Toad" - 171
Crossen, Dave - 169
Cullum, Dick - 60
Currier, Ken - 20, 163

D

Daddio, Bill - 11
Daley, Bill - 24, 55
Davey, John - 33
Davis, Chucky - 139, 140
Davis, Ray - 163
Davis, Willie - 128
Dawkins, Joe - 107, 108
Dean, Ross - 75
DeCorrevont, Bill - 20
DeLisle, Jim - 110, 169
Dellenbach, Jeff - 162, 168
Derleth, Henry - 67, 70, 71, 77
Diercks, Bob - 23, 129
DiMaggio, Joe - 15
Dittrich, John - 130
Dixon, John - 161
Dobbs, Glenn - 128
Domres, Tom - 169
Doran, Mark - 137
Dornberg, Roger - 44-46
Dudley, Anthony - 132
Dugger, Jack - 33

E

Eason, Tony - 144
Egloff, Ron - 121
Eisenhower, Dwight - 66
Eller, Carl - 94
Elliott, Bump - 35
Elliott, Pete - 35
Ellis, Jerry - 47
Elser, Don - 95
Embach, Jim - 38, 40
Emery, Larry - 173, 174
Erickson, John - 81
Esser, Clarence - 33, 129
Evans, Gene - 35, 38, 40
Evashevski, Forest - 54
Ezerins, Elmars - 93, 98, 99

F

Fabry, John - 74, 75, 91, 92
Farris, Tom - 129, 169
Faurot, Don - 20
Faverty, Hal - 44-46, 48, 129, 169
Fawley, Charlie - 175
Fekete, Gene - 21
Felker, Gene - 44, 48
Fenske, Chuck - 2
Ferguson, Bob - 69
Ferguson, Rufus "Roadrunner" - 32, 59, 109-115, 117, 118, 124, 151, 164, 168, 170, 181, 182
Fisher, Fritz - 81
Flemming, Neil - 74, 75, 77, 78
Foggie, Rickey - 173
Foster, Harold "Bud" - 2
Frain, Ron - 82, 100
Franck, George - 12, 128
Fredrick, Craig - 137, 138, 143
Fry, Hayden - 141

G

Gable, Bill - 40, 162, 163
Gage, Fred - 145
George, Wray - 31-33
Giel, Paul - 62, 63
Gillette, Eddie - 2, 5
Gipp, George - 65
Girard, Earl "Jug" - 2, 31-36, 38, 73, 75, 129, 170, 179, 181

Gladem, Wendell - 140, 141, 144
Goldberg, Marshall - 11, 16
Goldenberg, Charles - 168
Golemgeske, John - 129, 163
Gotta, John - 67, 163
Grabow, Brad - 145
Graff, Neil - 106-108, 110, 111, 171, 182
Graham, Otto - 23, 28, 129
Grange, Red - 2, 6
Grant, Bud - 40
Green, Charles - 132
Green, Dennis - 106, 107
Green, Gerald - 140, 146
Greenwood, David - 141, 169
Gregoire, Todd - 168, 173-175
Gregory, Bill - 110, 130, 169
Greyer, Neovia - 106, 107
Grimm, Dick - 91

H

Hable, Burt - 47, 48, 161
Hackbart, Dale - 65-71, 74-76, 78, 168-171, 181, 182
Hackett, Bill - 33
Haese, Jack - 33
Hake, Scott - 75
Halleran, Tim - 123
Haluska, Jim - 63, 73-78, 129, 161, 171
Ham, Jack - 110
Hammond, Jim - 44-46, 48
Hanzlik, Bob - 20
Harder, Pat - 2, 13, 15-24, 28, 29, 55, 75, 127-129, 167, 168, 170, 179
Harmon, Tom - 12, 60, 128
Harris, Dave - 111
Harris, Franco - 110
Harrison, Marck - 174, 175
Hart, Ed - 67, 70, 74
Havlicek, John - 81
Hayes, Jackie - 7
Hayes, Woody - 55, 69, 103
Heineke, Jim - 67, 74, 163
Hekkers, George - 129
Hellenbrand, Bill - 17
Henrici, Ron - 163
Hermann, Mark - 133, 138
Hilles, Jim - 134
Hirsbrunner, Paul - 19, 20, 163
Hirsch, Elroy "Crazylegs" - 2, 15, 18-25, 28, 29, 32, 52, 59, 60, 73-78, 104, 107, 117, 124, 127, 129, 130, 167-170, 176, 179, 181, 181
Hobbs, Billy - 74, 76, 77
Hobbs, Jon - 74, 76
Hoegh, Mark - 161
Hogan, Hulk - 33
Hohman, Jon - 100, 163
Holland, Lou - 83, 92-95, 98-100, 103, 163, 181
Holmes, Jim - 67
Holmes, Nick - 33
Holzwarth, Karl - 67-70, 74, 77
Hoover, Herbert - 6
Hornung, Paul - 65
Horvath, Les - 33
Hoskins, Mark - 10, 19, 23, 24, 27-30, 182
Houdini, Harry - 64, 117
Hovland, Lynn - 129
Howard, Dave - 74, 77
Howard, Larry - 98, 100
Howard, Mike - 157, 173-175
Howey, Greg - 92
Huarte, John - 89
Hutchinson, Billy - 47, 182
Huxhold, Ken - 40, 75, 162, 168
Huxhold, Terry - 67

I

Isbell, Cecil - 10, 128

J

Jackson, Fred - 157
Jacobazzi, Roger - 92, 100, 163
Jaeger, Roger - 106, 107, 110, 111
James, Tom - 21
Jankowski, Eddie - 9-13, 15, 55, 129
Janowicz, Vic - 46, 60
Jardine, Dan - 177
Jardine, John - 67, 69, 70, 110, 111, 113, 119, 121-124, 131, 135, 164, 176, 177, 180
Jardine, Len - 69
Jenkins, Lowell - 67, 163
Joesting, Herb - 55
Johnson, Bob - 117, 118, 121, 162
Johnson, Charley - 43
Johnson, Farnham - 20
Johnson, Greg - 151
Johnson, Lawrence - 169
Johnson, Richard - 169, 174
Jones, Ernie - 99
Jones, Michael - 143- 147
Jones, Robert - 95
Jones, Tom - 6

Jordan, Lynn - 10, 163
Josten, John - 132, 134, 137
Jurgensen, Sonny - 32

K

Kabat, Greg - 9, 163, 168
Kalasmiki, Mike - 131-135
Karras, Johnny - 46, 60
Karsatos, Jim - 175
Keeler, Tubby - 169
Kellogg, Bill - 74, 77
Kelly, Joe - 40, 162
Kempthorne, Dion - 100, 163
Kennedy, Bob - 44, 169
Kimball, Larry - 105
Kindt, Don - 2, 75, 171, 181
King, Troy - 135, 137, 138, 143, 147, 162
Kinnick, Nile - 11, 12
Kinzer, Matt - 146
Klinkhammer, Dan - 77
Klosek, Tim - 176
Knauff, Don - 40, 162
Knight, Bob - 81
Kobza, Bob - 148, 175
Kocourek, Dave - 74, 76
Koeck, Rich - 117, 118, 121, 162
Kostka, Stan - 55
Kotz, John - 2
Kramer, Jerry - 85
Kreick, Ray - 182
Kroner, Gary - 83, 84, 93-95, 97, 99, 100, 163
Krumrie, Tim - 134, 137, 140, 141, 145, 147, 163-165, 168, 181
Kuechle, Oliver - 59, 60
Kulcinski, Jerry - 67, 163
Kurek, Ralph - 15, 84, 92, 95, 96, 98, 100, 163

L

Lamia, Vince - 168
Lamphere, Bob - 46
Lane, Bill - 44
Lanphaer, Dan - 67, 69, 74, 163, 167, 168
Lanphaer, George - 48, 51
Laubenheimer, Roger - 33
Layne, Bobby - 32
Leafblad, Ron - 84, 94, 100
Leahy, Frank - 20
Leu, Bob - 44
Levenhagen, Jill - 7
Levenick, Dave - 141
LeVoir, Babe - 55
Lewis, Danny - 74, 76, 77
Lick, Dennis - 117, 118, 129, 162, 168, 179
Lick, Steve - 117, 118
Lindberg, Les - 163
Linfor, Joe - 7
Lokanc, Dave - 113
Lombardi, Vince - 89, 92
Lopp, Frank - 129
Lowe, Billy - 182
Lowell, Richard "Bud" - 75
Lowman, Guy - 79
Lucas, Jerry - 81
Luckman, Sid - 128
Luisetti, Hank - 154
Lund, Pug - 7
Lyons, Pat - 20, 24

M

Mack, Jeff - 113, 119, 182
Mahnke, Al - 163
Makris, George - 24
Manders, Jack - 7
Mansfield, Arthur - 37, 66, 81
Mantle, Mickey - 154
Marek, Billy - 32, 59, 117-125, 131, 155, 156, 162, 163, 168, 179, 181
Marks, Randy - 106, 107
Marrow, Brian - 148
Marsh, Fred - 48
Martin, Charles - 123
Martin, George - 105
Martine, Jim - 135
Matthews, Ira - 123, 132, 133, 182
Maves, Earl - 35, 38, 129
McAfee, George - 128
McBride, Chuck - 163
McCauley, Tom - 104, 156
McClain, Dave - 69, 131, 132, 134, 135, 137, 138, 140, 144-146, 148, 155-157, 164, 173, 175-177
McClain, Judy - 176
McCormick, Henry J. - 5, 37, 45, 55
McDowell, Layne - 162
McFadden, Thad - 137, 139, 141, 174
McFadzean, Jim - 24
McGee, Max - 85
McGlynn, Stoney - 21
McGuire, Mickey - 2, 5-9, 168, 170, 180, 181
McKay, Bob - 24
McKay, John - 98

McKinney, Jerry - 75, 78
McMillin, Bo - 33
McMillin, Jim - 163
Mead, Jack - 33, 34, 129
Meanwell, Walter "Doc" - 27
Mehl, Walter - 2
Melka, Jim - 146, 169, 182
Messner, Gary - 51, 54, 56, 168, 170
Meunier, Dick - 76
Meyer, Martin - 33
Meyers, Tilden - 40
Mialik, Larry - 110, 111, 182
Miller, Jim - 63, 171, 182
Miller, Paul - 10
Miller, Ron - 80, 91, 92, 171
Mitchell, Lydell - 110
Mohapp, Dave - 15, 135, 137, 140
Molinaro, Cappy - 7
Molinaro, Frank "Moon" - 6-8, 163
Moll, Keckie - 2
Moore, Brian - 67
Morgan, Mike - 123
Morrow, Archie - 75
Motl, Kevin - 134
Mott, Jim - 65
Mucks, Arlie Sr. - 5, 167
Mueller, Herbert "Butch" - 80
Murray, Jack - 168
Myers, Tom - 83

N

Nagurski, Bronko - 2, 55
Nathenson, Bill - 170
Nault, Jeff - 141, 144
Neal, Marvin - 139, 140
Negus, Fred - 20, 24, 75, 129, 163, 170
Nelson, Bob - 67, 163
Nettles, Jim - 84, 95, 100, 169, 182
Nevers, Ernie - 6
Nomellini, Leo - 40
Norvell, Merritt - 75, 100
Norwick, Joe - 117, 118, 121, 162
Nosbusch, Keith - 113
Novak, Jack - 121

O

O'Brien, John "Blackie" - 163
O'Brien, Pat - 112
O'Dea, Pat - 2, 5, 9, 168
O'Donahue, Pat - 43-45, 48, 49, 85, 129, 168, 181
Odson, Urban - 12
O'Rourke, Charley - 128
Ortman, Chuck - 60
Otterback, Hal - 40, 162
Owens, Steve - 105

P

Pacetti, Mario - 163
Parish, Steve - 134
Parseghian, Ara - 70, 83
Partenheimer, Irv - 74, 76
Paskvan, George - 9-13, 15, 55, 129
Paterno, Joe - 110
Patrick, J. D. - 145
Peabody, Alvin - 113
Pearson, Bret - 146, 182
Perkins, Ron - 67, 163
Perkovich, Jack - 94
Peters, Kent - 47
Petruska, Bob - 40, 171
Pillath, Roger - 92, 100, 130, 163
Piraino, Al - 92
Pollard, Ron - 119, 123
Powers, Francis - 19, 21
Prchlik, Art - 161
Pukema, Helge - 12
Purnell, Jim - 99, 100, 169

Q

Quaerna, Arnie - 91
Quirk, Richard - 7

R

Raddatz, Craig - 174-176
Rainsberger, Ellis - 123
Ralls, Glen - 80
Ray, Bob - 20, 21, 23
Rebholz, Hal - 2
Reddick, Mel - 105-107
Rehm, Fred - 21
Reichardt, Bill - 48
Reichardt, Rick - 100
Reid, Michael - 174, 175
Reimer, John - 117, 118, 121, 162
Relich, Dan - 123
Rennebohm, Bob - 35, 38, 75

Rice, Eric - 104
Richardson, Chuck - 113
Richter, Bob - 104
Richter, Pat - 67, 79-87, 90, 91, 93-96, 99-101, 127-129, 156, 167-169, 177, 179, 181
Richter, Pat Sr. - 67, 80
Roberts, John - 24, 163
Robinson, Jackie - 128
Rockne, Knute - 10, 20, 85, 112
Rogers, Jim - 67
Rohde, Kevin - 146, 147
Ronzani, Gene - 7
Roosevelt, Franklin D. - 6
Rundle, Dick - 144

S

Sachtjen, Ken - 40
Sarringhaus, Paul - 21
Scesniak, Dick - 176
Schade, Don - 67
Schembechler, Bo - 122
Schenk, Jim - 92, 99, 100, 163
Schiller, Bob - 7
Schleissner, Bill - 47
Schlichter, Art - 141
Schmitz, Bill - 11
Schoonover, Al - 67, 70, 71
Schrader, Dave - 111
Schreiner, Dave - 12, 18, 19-22, 24, 27-30, 167, 168, 169, 179, 181
Seamonson, Al - 140
Seelinger, Bud - 23, 28, 182
Seifert, Mike - 111
Seiler, Jay - 134, 176
Self, Clarence - 35
Severson, Pete - 162
Shafer, Allen - 34
Shaw, Bob - 21
Shawaiko, Paul - 74, 75, 77, 78
Shloredt, Bob - 71
Shumate, Mark - 147
Silvestri, Carl - 100, 103, 171
Simkowski, George - 161
Simmons, Ken - 168
Simpson, O.J. - 53
Sims, Clint - 146
Sims, Darryl - 147, 168
Skavarka, Bernie - 46
Smart, James H. - 1
Smith, Billy - 94, 100
Smith, Bruce - 12, 17, 20
Smith, Jerry - 44-46, 48
Smith, Red - 52
Smith, Ron - 82, 93, 99, 100
Smith, Steve - 139, 140
Smith, Willie Ray - 82
Snell, Matt - 103
Snell, Ray - 135, 168
Snypp, Wilbur - 103
Soltau, Gordy - 40
Souza, Wayne - 134, 176
Spangler, Rich - 175
Spears, Clarence "Doc" - 7, 9, 10, 27
Spencer, Tim - 140
Spielman, Chris - 175
Spurlin, Larry - 152
Stalcup, Jerry "Sparky" - 67, 69, 130, 163, 168
Staley, Ron - 74, 75
Starch, Ken - 15, 119, 120, 123
Stargell, Willie - 66
Stauss, Tom - 132, 133, 135
Stebbins, Harold "Curly" - 11
Stein, Ed - 91
Steiner, Ron - 67, 69, 70, 74, 75, 78
Steinmetz, George - 161, 162
Stensby, Clarence - 161, 162
Stern, Bill - 32
Stieve, Terry - 117, 118, 121, 162, 168
Stills, Ken - 175, 177
Stock, Mike - 70, 123
Stoll, Cal - 133
Stoltz, Denny - 120
Stracka, Tim - 132, 147, 156, 182
Strehlow, Rollie - 44, 46-48
Stueck, Lew - 122
Stuhldreher, Harry - 2, 9-12, 18, 20, 21, 21, 24, 27-29, 35, 37-39, 162
Stupka, Bob - 24
Subach, Mark - 145, 162
Suminski, Dave - 161
Sundt, Guy - 40, 55

T

Taggart, Ed - 175
Taliaferro, George - 38
Tarkenton, Fran - 101
Taylor, Bobby - 173
Teague, Bob - 40, 162
Telander, Rick - 67
Tennant, John - 12, 169, 182
Temp, Jim - 129, 169
Teteak, Deral - 44, 45, 48, 169

Thistlewaite, Glenn - 170
Thompson, Alan "A-Train" - 15, 105-108, 110, 111, 151
Thompson, Jerry - 2, 33, 34
Thornally, Dick - 24, 163
Tobias, Dave "Moose" - 6-8
Todd, Wayne - 104
Tomczak, Mike - 174
Tonnemaker, Clayton - 40
Toon, Al - 144, 146-148, 151, 155-159, 168, 169, 174, 175, 181, 182
Tringali, John - 176
Trippi, Charley - 16
Turner, L. Roger - 145

U

Underwood, Steve - 79, 85, 90-92, 99, 100, 163
Ursin, Don - 161

V

Vanden Boom, Matt - 140, 141, 147, 169
Vander Kelen, Ron - 74, 77, 80, 81, 83-85, 89-101, 127-129, 133, 155, 163, 167, 168, 179-181
Van Dyke, LaVern - 64, 109-110
Val Galder, Clark - 65-66
Veith, Steve - 135
Versich, Collin - 94
Versnik, Ron - 139, 145, 162
Vinje, Art - 33
Vogds, Evan - 20, 129, 163
Voigt, Stu - 107, 108, 168
Von Heimburg, Ernie - 99, 100, 163
Voss, Don - 44, 47, 161, 168

W

Wagner, Steve - 122, 129, 169
Walker, Carlton - 139, 177
Walker, Elbert - 110
Walker, Melvin - 177
Walsh, John - 2, 55, 56
Ward, Arch - 127
Warfield, Paul - 93
Warmath, Murray - 84, 94, 95
Washington, Selvie - 119
Wasserbach, Lloyd - 20, 24, 163
Waterfield, Bob - 154
Webster, Mike - 113, 117, 129, 163-165, 168, 170, 179
Weisenberger, Jack - 35
Weiss, Howie - 9-13, 15, 27, 55, 129
Wesley, Jim - 113
Westphal, Fred - 152
Westphal, John "Stony" - 151-154
White, Bob - 69
White, Lorenzo - 176
Whittenton, Jesse - 85, 101, 129
Wiesner, Tom - 67, 69, 71, 74, 75, 77
Wildung, Dick - 12, 17
Wilkinson, Bud - 39
Williams, John - 137, 139, 140, 144, 145, 182
Williams, Sidney - 74, 76
Williams, Ted - 15
Williamson, Ivan - 7, 37, 39-41, 43, 45, 48, 51, 55, 60, 63, 64, 103, 162, 176
Willis, Bill - 33
Wilson, Ben - 98
Wilson, David - 138
Wilson, Glen - 76
Wilson, Robert "Red" - 35, 37-41, 162, 167-170, 179
Winchell, Walter - 10
Winckler, Bob - 139, 145, 162
Winfrey, Chuck - 110
Wink, Jack - 18, 20, 21, 29, 38, 169, 171, 182
Wistert, Alvin - 35
Withers, Ed - 44, 45, 169
Witt, Jerry - 44, 46-48
Wojdula, Andy - 100
Woodson, Rod - 147, 155
Woolfolk, Butch - 139
Wright, Randy - 141, 143-149, 155, 156, 168, 182

Y

Yerges, Howard - 35
Young, Francis "Shorty" - 74, 77
Young, Steve - 163

Z

Zeimetz, Art - 121
Zeman, Bob - 67, 69, 71, 169
Zouvas, Pete - 67, 163

PHOTO CREDITS

Page 1-Top	University of Wisconsin
Page 1-Bottom	State Historical Society of Wisconsin-Vinje Collection
Page 2-Upper left	State Historical Society of Wisconsin-Vinje Collection
Page 2-Upper right	University of Wisconsin
Page 2-Bottom	University of Wisconsin
Page 3	Illustration by Jeff Butler
Page 4-Top	Unknown
Page 4-Bottom	University of Wisconsin
Page 5	Wisconsin State Journal
Page 6-Top	University of Wisconsin
Page 6-Bottom	Wisconsin State Journal-Edwin Stein
Page 7	Wisconsin State Journal
page 8-Upper left	University of Wisconsin
Page 8-Upper right	University of Wisconsin
Page 8-Bottom	University of Wisconsin
Page 9	University of Wisconsin
Page 10-Top	University of Wisconsin
Page 10-Bottom	University of Wisconsin
Page 11	Wisconsin State Journal-L. Roger Turner
Page 12-Upper left	Wisconsin State Journal-J.D. Patrick
Page 12-Upper right	Wisconsin State Journal-J.D. Patrick
Page 12-Bottom	Wisconsin State Journal-Edwin Stein
Page 13-Top	Associated Press
Page 13-Bottom	University of Wisconsin
Page 14-Top	Wisconsin State Journal-L. Roger Turner
Page 14-Bottom	Wisconsin State Journal-J.D. Patrick
Page 15	University of Wisconsin
Page 16	Associated Press